Richard Vargoshe, D.V.M., graduated from the New York State School of Veterinary Medicine, Cornell, in 1949 and has had more than thirty years of uninterrupted experience in the field of animal medicine. He currently has offices in New York City, Woodbury, Connecticut, and Block Island.

Peter Steinberg is a full-time writer who resides in New York City. He is the author of *Roller Babies*, also published by Prentice-Hall.

THE
HOUSEHOLD BOOK
OF
ANIMAL MEDICINE

Richard Vargoshe D.V.M.
Peter Steinberg

A SPECTRUM BOOK

PRENTICE-HALL, INC.
Englewood Cliffs, New Jersey 07632

Library of Congress Cataloging in Publication Data

VARGOSHE, RICHARD.
   The household book of animal medicine.

   (A Spectrum Book)
   Includes index.
   1. Pets—Diseases.   2. Veterinary medicine.
I. Steinberg, Peter, joint author.   II. Title.
SF981.V37   636.089   80-36733
ISBN 0-13-395871-X
ISBN 0-13-395863-9 (pbk.)

© 1980 by Peter Steinberg and Richard Vargoshe.

A SPECTRUM BOOK

10 9 8 7 6 5 4 3 2 1

Printed in the United States of America

Editorial/production supervision and interior design by Frank Moorman
Manufacturing buyer: Barbara A. Frick

PRENTICE-HALL INTERNATIONAL, INC., *London*
PRENTICE-HALL OF AUSTRALIA PTY. LIMITED, *Sydney*
PRENTICE-HALL OF CANADA, LTD., *Toronto*
PRENTICE-HALL OF INDIA PRIVATE LIMITED, *New Delhi*
PRENTICE-HALL OF JAPAN, INC., *Tokyo*
PRENTICE-HALL OF SOUTHEAST ASIA PTE. LTD., *Singapore*
WHITEHALL BOOKS LIMITED, *Wellington, New Zealand*

Contents

How to Use this Book   1

SYMPTOMS   3
Symptoms of Broken Bones   5
Symptoms of Burns   7
Symptoms of Common Wounds   9
Symptoms of Constipation   11
Dental Conditions   12
Symptoms of Diarrhea   14
Symptoms of External Parasites   15
The Birth Cycle   17
Symptoms of Internal Parasites   19
Symptoms of Serious Diseases   24
Symptoms of Skin Diseases and Disorders   27
Symptoms of Sprains   29
Symptoms of Good and Bad Nutrition   30

DIAGNOSIS AND TREATMENT 33

Broken Bones 35
Burns 41
Common Wounds 48
Constipation 55
Dental Care 61
Diarrhea 68
External Parasites 73
Giving Birth 79
Internal Parasites 90
Respiratory Infections 101
Serious Diseases 107
Skin Diseases and Disorders 115
Sprains 121
Vitamins and Food Requirements 126

OVER-THE-COUNTER MEDICINES 133

Prescription for Broken Bones 135
Prescription for Burns 137
Prescription for Common Wounds 140
Prescription for Constipation 143
Prescription for Dental Care 145
Prescription for Diarrhea 146
Prescription for External Parasites 148
Prescription for the Birth Cycle 150
Prescription for Internal Parasites 151
Prescription for Respiratory Infections 153
Prescription for Serious Diseases 156
Prescription for Skin Diseases and Disorders 157
Prescription for Sprains 159
Prescription for Vitamin and Food Requirements 161

HOUSEHOLD PETS 163

Your Veterinarian 165
How to Use Your Pet Store 168
Basic Pet Care 173

BIRDS, FISH, AND TURTLES   183

Birds   185
Fresh-Water Tropical Fish   195
Turtles   203

INDEX   211

DEDICATION   For Evelyn Vargoshe
and Henry Orensten

ACKNOWL-   Richard Jupa and Vikki Orenstein for able assistance in composi-
EDGMENTS   tion and research.

Neil Lazarine, Ph.D., for arduous and persistent research.

Kathy Talebian and Studio 305 for prompt copying services.

Irving Zimmerman, D.V.M. (and office staff) for constant encour-
agement and good wishes.

And thank you to these pet shops for their help in marketing this
book and providing information when it was needed:

Laila Stellmah and Susan Bishop of Deer–Run Kennels, Ltd.

Bob Manney of The Menagerie.

Dick Ibling of Pets Unlimited.

Elly Kuranuki and Roosevelt Baker of The West Side Pet Shop.

How to Use This Book

When your pet is sick or in pain, you will want to help it quickly and with a minimum of fuss; and *The Household Book of Animal Medicine* has been especially designed to do just that.

Most of the book concerns dogs and cats and the common ailments that can affect them. The material has been divided into fourteen chapters, and each chapter further broken down into three easy reference sections, so you will not have to wade through a lot of unnecessary information to find what you need.

The first section, "Symptoms," will help you to identify your animal's problem. Next, "Diagnosis and Treatment," explains each condition and offers various modes of treatment. The third section is "Over-the-Counter Medicines"; if the recommended treatment (for any ailment) includes nonprescription medication, this section will provide complete instruction on its usage.

Everything has been organized for convenience and ease of access. Each section is preceeded by a separate table of contents, and the fourteen chapters in each section have been cross-indexed with their corresponding chapters in the other sections. On the first page of any chapter, you will find an easy-reference index box. The information inside the box will direct you to the corresponding chapters in other sections. For example, if you are looking up the symptoms for "Broken Bones," the index box will give you the page numbers for "Diagnosis and Treatment," and "Over-the-Counter Medicines" for the same condition. You can read only the section that you are immediately concerned with, or you can absorb all of the material on any specific ailment.

The remainder of this book is divided into two sections of special interest. The first provides informational chapters on "Your Veterinarian," "How to Use Your Pet Store," and "Basic Pet Care"; and the second discusses "Birds," "Fresh-Water Tropical Fish," and "Turtles." Both of these sections are preceded by a separate table of contents.

SYMPTOMS

Symptoms of Broken Bones 5
Symptoms of Burns 7
Symptoms of Common Wounds 9
Symptoms of Constipation 11
Dental Conditions 12
Symptoms of Diarrhea 14
Symptoms of External Parasites 15
The Birth Cycle 17
Symptoms of Internal Parasites 19
Symptoms of Serious Diseases 24
Symptoms of Skin Diseases and Disorders 27
Symptoms of Sprains 29
Symptoms of Good and Bad Nutrition 30

If you are unable to identify your pet's condition, you should look through this section first. Check your animal's symptoms against those that are given for each specific ailment.

Even if you are already aware of the condition that is affecting your pet, you may still want to turn to the appropriate chapter to confirm your evaluation.

Symptoms of Broken Bones

For further information, see:
Diagnosis and Treatment   35
Over-the-Counter Medicines   135

Animals with broken bones will be in great pain and discomfort. They will usually cry or bite when you touch the affected area or attempt to pick them up. If they have fractured a limb, they will tend to lie around, and in some cases they will even lie on the injured part.

Fractures will generally not bear weight or pressure, and in most cases the animal will not walk if one of its bones is broken.

Additionally, the area around the fracture will swell within twenty-four hours after the break. This swelling is extremely painful, and the animal will usually show signs of great distress.

Sometimes the fracture will be obvious. Broken legs and forearms, for example, may be twisted, distorted, or may flop loosely about. These injuries will not bear weight, so if your pet is limping, it is probably not a fracture. Wait for two or three days to see if the limping improves before consulting your veterinarian.

In some cases you will be able to see the jagged end or ends of the broken bone because it has pushed through the animal's skin. These fractures are called compound, as opposed to simple fractures where the pieces of the broken bone remain inside the animal's body.

Sometimes the fracture will not be immediately obvious. Small dogs and cats, for example, may be able to walk on a broken pelvis. If your pet has been injured, look for swelling around the injured area. If the area is swollen and painful to your touch, it may be due to a broken bone. If the condition does not improve within twenty-four hours, see your veterinarian.

Symptoms of Burns

For further information, see:
Diagnosis and Treatment   47
Over-the-Counter Medicines   137

There are three distinctly separate kinds of burns that can affect your pet—electrical, thermal, and friction. Each of these burns will cause definite (but different) symptoms, and this will enable the pet-owner to make a prompt diagnosis and begin treatment.

Electrical burns are the most dangerous kind of burn, because pets are often jolted into a cardiac arrest (and die) before they can be treated. The burn itself is usually characterized by seared flesh, reddened skin, and lesions or blisters. The area that encompasses the burn will almost always be painful to your touch; there are other symptoms, too.

Affected pets can display respiratory distress, and they may appear to be pale or blue, especially in their lips, gums, and the lining of their eyelids. The animal can also develop rigidity in its limbs. It may have a glassy stare, and in some cases, the animal can even collapse.

WARNING A heavy jolt of electricity can cause animals (that live through it) to go into shock. Shock will cause pets to lose color in their lips and gums (and other mucous membranes). Affected animals will also lose body heat, and their temperatures will begin to drop significantly.*

Thermal burns will be readily visible on the animal's skin. The area around the burn will usually be singed or charred, and any exposed skin will be reddened or inflamed. In severe cases, the area can be blistered, as well. If you touch the wound, it will feel warm or hot. But thermal burns can be quite painful, and your pet may resist when you attempt to touch the injured spot.

Friction burns cause symptoms that at first appear to be only marginally different than those that are caused by thermal burns. But if you look closely, you will be able to tell them apart.

Instead of singed or charred skin, the region around the burn will appear to be scraped or chafed, and there will be resultant bare spots. The bare skin will usually be rubbed raw, and may also be red, irritated, or inflamed. Because these burns are usually caused by a related trauma, you may also see cuts and lacerations, or particles of foreign material imbedded in the animal's skin. As in other burns, the area may be painful to your touch.

*Shock is very serious, and it should be treated without delay. If you believe your pet to be in shock, keep it warm and see your veterinarian immediately! For additional information, see "Diagnosis and Treatment" (electrical burns).

Symptoms of Common Wounds

For further information, see:
Diagnosis and Treatment   48
Over-the-Counter Medicines   140

Animals can suffer a number of common wounds from a variety of causes. It is important to recognize and treat these wounds as soon as possible. Four of the most common wounds are cuts, lacerations, abrasions, and bruises. Here are the symptoms to look for.

Cuts are normally characterized by tissue that has been smoothly separated. The cut may also be accompanied by bleeding.

Lacerations can be identified by tissue that has been torn, rather than smoothly separated as in cuts. The tear may also be accompanied by bleeding, swelling, irritation of the surrounding area, and black or blue discoloration on the animal's skin.

Abrasions are characterized by tissue that has been rubbed or scraped bare of its outer layers. The animal may also exhibit pain, swelling, redness, and heat in the area of the injury.

Bruises are also called contusions, and they can be easily recognized. Look for black-and-blue tissue. Additionally, the injured area may begin to swell, but there will usually be no separation or tear in the animal's tissue.

Symptoms of Constipation

For further information, see:
Diagnosis and Treatment 55
Over-the-Counter Medicines 143

You will have to observe your pet during a bowel movement before you can determine whether or not it is constipated.

If your animal struggles and strains during a bowel movement without passing stool, it is probably constipated.

It is important, however, to be able to differentiate between constipation and diarrhea. If your animal strains and passes a small amount of liquid or very soft, mushy stool, it has diarrhea. Turn to the proper section on diarrhea for diagnosis and treatment.

Secondary Symptoms A constipated animal usually avoids food and any attempts to feed it.

Constipated animals may also undergo a slight change in personality, becoming more nervous or irritable than normal.

Symptoms of Dental Conditions

For further information, see:
Diagnosis and Treatment   61
Over-the-Counter Medicines   145

If your pet is bothered by problems with its teeth or gums, it will probably display symptoms of neglect or disease. These symptoms are often visible to the human eye. If you suspect a dental problem is affecting your dog or cat, look for any of the following indications:

Affected animals may exhibit large areas of tartar on their tooth enamel. Tartar is a brownish incrustation that first begins to accumulate at the animal's gum line. This condition can be mild or quite severe. In addition to this incrustation, cats will frequently display eroded enamel.

Besides tartar, you may see particles of bone fragments or other foreign materials wedged between your pet's upper teeth (across the roof of its mouth). Or you may see small deposits of food particles or hair starting to accumulate on the teeth. If unattended, these deposits can develop into tartar.

In most cases, the affected animal will have bad breath and you will easily be able to smell this symptom. Bad breath can be common in dental problems, and this symptom will almost always accompany any of the other symptoms for bad teeth and gums.

There are also some infections and diseases that can affect your animal's dental health. These conditions will usually produce specific symptoms.

Animals that suffer bad teeth from mouth or throat infections will usually cough or discharge substance from their nose or mouth. They will almost always suffer from bad breath, and they may also display any of the visible symptoms, like excess tartar.

Gingivitis is a disease that often develops from extremely dirty teeth and accumulated tartar. This disease can erode your pet's enamel, inflame its gums, and loosen its teeth. Your animal may also have bad breath. This condition will eventually cause your pet to lose its teeth, either naturally or by extraction.

Organic diseases like uremia can also lead to dental problems. This condition originates in the animal's kidneys. The teeth can be incrusted, often displaying a blackish tartar. The animal will usually have bad breath. Also, because the animal's kidneys are not functioning properly, the pet will suffer an extraordinary thirst and may drink repeatedly in order to quench it.

WARNING   When young animals are teething, they will sometimes chew on hard, wood objects (like chair legs) or on bones. During the chewing process, these hard objects may fragment, and small chips may be swallowed, often causing conditions like diarrhea or constipation. The affected animal may exhibit symptoms of pain or distress and begin to vomit. If the condition persists, or if the symptoms are unusually severe, you should consult your veterinarian.

Symptoms of Diarrhea

For further information, see:
Diagnosis and Treatment   68
Over-the-Counter Medicines   146

When your pet is suffering from diarrhea, you will recognize it immediately. Look at a recent stool. If the stool is liquid, it is a sure indication of diarrhea.

The stool may also be an abnormal color, but this is not normally a sign of danger. However, if there is blood in the stool, you should consult your veterinarian.

Symptoms of External Parasites

For further information, see:
Diagnosis and Treatment   73
Over-the-Counter Medicines   148

There are several types of external parasites that will be visible on your animal's body. Fleas, ticks, lice, and maggots are all easily recognized.

- *Fleas* are tiny brown bugs that can often be viewed moving rapidly through your pet's coat.
- *Ticks* are small, round, dark bugs with hard, external shells. They will not appear to move once they have attached themselves to an animal's body.
- *Lice* are small, dark grey bugs that appear to be stationary on your animal's body.
- *Maggots* are a larval form of blow flies, resembling tiny worms.

These parasites will sometimes cause your pet to suffer related skin conditions with uncomfortable symptoms like scratching and hair loss. See "Skin Diseases and Disorders" for diagnosis and treatment.

Some types of external parasites, specifically mites, cannot be seen by the human eye and will require a microscopic examination by your veterinarian before they can be detected and treated.

This group includes sarcoptic, demodectic, and ear mites. Sarcoptic and demodectic mites will always cause related skin conditions in affected animals. Ear mites will generally cause inflammation and/or irritation inside your pet's ears.

If your animal's skin condition fails to respond to treatment, or if it improves and later reappears, see your veterinarian. Your pet may be infested by microscopic mites that will need professional attention before they can be eliminated. Also, if you suspect ear mites, see your veterinarian.

The Birth Cycle

For further information, see:
Diagnosis and Treatment   79
Over-the-Counter Medicines   150

A female dog or cat will display specific symptoms throughout the reproductive cycle. These symptoms will indicate when she is in heat (the period before pregnancy) and when she is actually pregnant. Some of these symptoms will persist through gestation, and you may even know when the birth is imminent.

Heat   When a dog is in heat, her vulva will swell and she will periodically release a bloody discharge through it. There may be a large quantity of blood, or it may be barely noticeable. This symptom will continue to be present throughout heat.

Cats will often be nervous and jittery. They can roll back and forth and make a lot of noise. If your pet is in heat, she may lose her appetite, or she may begin to tread the ground nervously with her hind legs. Cats in heat will sometimes spray urine outside of the litter box. There can be many possible symptoms so you will have to know your own cat.

Pregnancy   Once female dogs or cats have mated, they will enter into pregnancy. Their bellies will swell progressively larger and they will begin and continue to develop their breasts. Dogs will start to build a nest (with newspapers, etc.) approximately twenty-four hours before they deliver their babies. Both dogs and cats will suddenly become very quiet in the moments immediately prior to the actual birth. This quiet is usually a symptom of the beginning of labor. The expectant mother will now experience contractions until her offspring are born.

Symptoms of Internal Parasites

For further information, see:
Diagnosis and Treatment   90
Over-the-Counter Medicines   151

There are several types of internal parasites that can inhabit your dog or cat, but the symptoms are not always obvious. For example, infestation can cause the affected animal to suffer from diarrhea, but pet-owners rarely associate diarrhea with internal parasites unless they have been previously alerted. The danger is that owners often (and mistakenly) treat the symptom instead of the cause, thereby prolonging their pet's condition instead of relieving it.

In general, these parasites will drain their victim's natural defenses, making the pet more susceptible to disease and infection. Heavily infested animals may lose their appetites and become lethargic. But these symptoms can also be confusing and hard to confirm.

Fortunately, many of these parasites produce specific indications of their presence, but you will have to know exactly what to look for. In most cases, a positive diagnosis can only be effected through a microscopic analysis of the animal's stool. So if you suspect infestation, consult your veterinarian.

These are the internal parasites that can affect your animal and the symptoms that each one will produce. Only two of these invaders (tapeworms and roundworms) will be readily visible to the human eye.

Tapeworms will leave visible segments of themselves in the animal's stool or in its regular sleeping place. They can also be seen under or around the animal's tail or near its anus. Look for tiny, lightly colored pieces of worm that roughly resemble rice kernels. Each worm part will be one-fourth of an inch to one inch long; although they eventually die from exposure to air, you may see some movement if they are still alive.

The animal can display the infestation in other ways, too. It can be sluggish and inactive, or it can eat more food and lose weight. Unfortunately, some animals will display no symptoms at all.

Roundworms (ascarids) look somewhat like small strands of spaghetti and can be seen in the stool or vomit of affected pets. These worms are two to four inches long, yellowish white in color, and have slightly pointed ends.

Affected animals often display listlessness, poor coats, and thin bodies. When younger animals are inhabited, their abdomens may swell after eating and be sensitive to the touch. Because roundworms travel to the lungs, severe infestations can result in pneumonia.

Hookworms are almost invisible to the naked eye and leave no observable evidence in the animal's stool. These worms can cause your pet to suffer from diarrhea (often with blood in it), cramps, pale gums, and pale lips. Infested animals may also have dry, unhealthy coats, a slight cough, and a noticeable weight loss.

In puppies (and also in mature animals with advanced infestations) hookworm can cause symptoms that resemble distemper—high fever, ill-smelling diarrhea, and a discharge from the animal's eyes and nostrils.

Whipworms often cause symptoms that are similar to those produced by hookworms. Affected animals can suffer from severe diarrhea (usually laced with blood), and they can also lose color in their mucous membranes (lips, gums, the lining of the eye lids). In some cases, the animal will suffer from an inflammation of the colon that will be sensitive to your touch.

Heartworms can plug your pet's arteries and affect its heart, often resulting in great stress to the animal's system. This stress can cause your pet to tire easily and be listless. Infested animals will generally display poor coats and suffer weight loss. They will also cough and pant constantly, even in cool weather.

Coccidia are one-celled protozoa that can cause their victims to suffer from diarrhea, emaciation, and a discharge from their eyes and nose.

Toxoplasmosis is an internal infestation that affects primarily cats. It can be difficult to detect, because it may cause no visible symptoms at all.

Symptoms of Respiratory Infections

For further information, see:
Diagnosis and Treatment   101
Over-the-Counter Medicines   153

Even though there are many kinds of respiratory infections in animals, most of these infections will display similar symptoms.

In both mild and severe conditions, for example, the affected animal will usually sneeze, cough, or suffer from running eyes.

The more serious conditions may also produce lethargy, loss of appetite, or a purulent discharge from the animal's nose. If your pet exhibits any of these symptoms, you should see your veterinarian quickly.

Sometimes your pet will suffer from well-defined infections and you can look for specific symptoms. For example, if your pet has a bacterial infection like tonsillitis or laryngitis, it can suffer from swollen glands and have difficulty in swallowing. Laryngitis can also alter the tone of your animal's voice.

Other bacterial conditions such as rhinitis or sinusitis are often symptoms (in themselves) of a more serious infection. They can cause inflammation of the animal's nasal passages and inhibit its breathing.

Some respiratory conditions are chronic. The symptoms are usually recognizable and they will continue to reappear. Here are several examples.

If your dog or cat is affected by a sinus condition, its nasal passages can be congested, causing labored breathing. Also, the animal may snort or discharge substance from its nose.

If your pet has asthma, it will usually have extreme difficulty in breathing. It is not uncommon for affected animals to wheeze both when inhaling and when exhaling.

If your pet is being affected by an allergy, it may display skin symptoms, like hives or even a rash. Allergies can also cause congestion and difficulty in breathing.

WARNING   There are some respiratory conditions like rhinotracheitis and calici virus* that are extremely dangerous to cats. If your cat is running a high fever and is obviously *very* sick with a respiratory infection, see your veterinarian immediately.

*See "Serious Diseases" for further information.

Symptoms of Serious Diseases

For further information, see:
Diagnosis and Treatment   107
Over-the-Counter Medicines   156

There are many serious diseases to which dogs and cats are susceptible. They can cause the animal to suffer great pain, and even death. However, it is extremely likely that you will never have to use this chapter, because properly vaccinated pets will not normally be threatened by any of these diseases.

Some of these conditions will affect only dogs, and others can affect only cats. One disease, rabies, can be contracted by either dogs or cats. Many of the symptoms will be easy to spot, whereas others may be confusing because they can be caused by several different conditions. Here are the signs to look for.

Dogs   *Canine distemper* almost always causes dogs to suffer from acute diarrhea. They may also have a high fever, a purulent discharge from their eyes and nose, and a thickening of their foot pads. In some cases, the animal will cough and suffer from muscle twitching or even convulsions. This disease is usually accompanied by pneumonia.

Infectious canine hepatitis is usually characterized by a high temperature, marked depression, and a congestion of the dog's mucous membranes. The dog may also exhibit a total disinterest in food, although it can have an insatiable thirst.

Leptospirosis generally induces a high fever, depression, loss of appetite, and congestion in the whites of the animal's eyes. Your dog may also exhibit pain in walking (or a "tucked up" walk), jaundice, vomiting, or diarrhea.

Infectious Canine Tracheobronchitis will cause your dog to develop a high fever. It is also characterized by severe, dry, coughing spasms that can cause your pet to gag and bring up mucous.

Cats *Cat distemper* will cause your cat to have a high fever, severe depression, vomiting, and diarrhea. When young kittens have peracute distemper (develops very rapidly), they can die suddenly without ever displaying any of the symptoms.

Respiratory illnesses can be extremely difficult to diagnose because many of the various conditions can cause similar symptoms. Cats often suffer from two or more of these infections at the same time. Some of the common symptoms can be loss of appetite (with resulting dehydration), depression, and a fever. Your cat can also sneeze, cough, or suffer from ocular or nasal discharges.

Many of the respiratory conditions are common in dogs, too, and they have already been covered in "Respiratory Infections." Three of the most serious illnesses affect only cats. Here are the symptoms of these highly dangerous conditions.

Rhinotracheitis is usually characterized by fever, sneezing, loss of appetite, and dehydration. Your cat can also have a discharge from its eyes and nose. It may also suffer from congestion and a swelling in the membranes of its upper respiratory tract.

Calici virus can cause your cat to sneeze and to suffer from nasal and ocular discharges. This condition can also produce fever, depression, loss of appetite, and dehydration. Many cats will also develop ulcerations on their tongues.

Pneumonitis is an upper respiratory disease that generally causes cats to suffer from labored breathing, sneezing, coughing, snorting, wheezing, and listlessness. Affected cats may also suffer from a loss of body fluids, and they can develop unusually high temperatures.

Dogs and Cats

Rabies can affect either dogs or cats, and they can contract either of two types—dumb or furious. Both types will cause fever, refusal to eat, and an inability to swallow that often results in drooling. In addition, your pet may also develop encephalitis, sometimes with convulsions or paralysis.

In the furious type of rabies, the animal can attack anything that moves, including motor vehicles, people, and other animals. In the dumb type of rabies, the animal does not attack, but it will display all of the other symptoms.

Symptoms of Skin Diseases and Disorders

For further information, see:
Diagnosis and Treatment   115
Over-the-Counter Medicines   157

There are many causes for the different skin problems that can affect your dog or cat, but most of the symptoms will be similar, regardless of the specific condition.

If your pet suffers from a local condition, it will exhibit areas of inflammation or irritation. You may also see hairless patches of red, raw, or discolored skin.

The more serious conditions like moist eczema, wet dermatitis, and acute pruritis will display symptoms such as raw, oozing patches of hairless skin. The area may also be moist to your touch. In some cases you will be able to see pus or other signs of serious trouble. These disorders need immediate attention, and you should see your veterinarian.

Occasionally you will see or feel a lump on your animal's skin. You will have to watch it carefully. If it is a harmless bruise, scratch, or infection, it will probably recede within a few days. If not, your pet may have a dangerous tumor and you should see your veterinarian as soon as possible. If the growth proves to be malignant, it will have to be removed.

Because tumors cannot be treated at home, and because they are so potentially dangerous, they will not be discussed in "Diagnosis and Treatment." See your veterinarian!

If your pet suffers from a symmetrical condition, both sides of its body will display equal symptoms. Most of the time you will be able to feel the symptoms as well as see them. For example, dry, dandruffy skin will be evident when you rub your animal's coat.

A generalized condition will exhibit the same symptoms all over your animal's body. A good example is seborrhea. If your pet is affected, its entire coat will be excessively oily or have dry encrustations.

Secondary
Symptoms

If your pet is constantly biting, licking, or scratching a particular area of its body, look for signs of skin trouble.

In cases of generalized problems, your animal will repeatedly bite or scratch all over its body.

Symptoms of Sprains

For further information, see:
Diagnosis and Treatment   121
Over-the-Counter Medicines   159

Sprains are wrenching injuries that affect joints, and they almost always occur in one of the animal's limbs. They can be very painful, and injured pets will usually display their distress. The sprain itself will also produce definite symptoms.

Look for rapid and continued swelling in the region of the injury. Some pets will be resistant when they are picked up or handled, but if you touch the swollen joint, it will feel warm or hot. As most sprains are in a limb, the animal will probably be unable to walk normally. It may limp, keep the injured limb from touching the ground, or it may not move at all.

Symptoms of
Good and Bad Nutrition

For further information, see:
Diagnosis and Treatment   126
Over-the-Counter Medicines   161

One of the best ways to keep your pet healthy is to feed it well-balanced and nutritious meals. If your dog or cat has a good diet, it will usually have bright, alert eyes, a smooth and glossy coat, a well-proportioned, slender frame, and a playful and active nature.

But if your pet is suffering from a general malnutrition, it can exhibit obvious and disquieting symptoms. Affected animals may have a thin and lackluster coat, a swollen belly and spindly legs, dull eyes, and dandruff.

Malnutrition can also cause your pet to suffer from specific diseases, like rickets and arthritis, and cats can also contract steatitis. These conditions will normally cause your animal to develop specific symptoms. Here are the signs to look for.

- *Rickets* will bend the bones of affected pets, and the bones or joints will usually appear to be bowed while the animal is walking.

- *Arthritis* will generally cause the affected animal to have difficulty in moving about; the animal may also whimper in pain or favor one of its legs while walking.
- *Steatitis* is normally characterized by a high fever, and the cat will also display obvious signs of distress and pain.

DIAGNOSIS AND TREATMENT

Broken Bones	35
Burns	41
Common Wounds	48
Constipation	55
Dental Care	61
Diarrhea	68
External Parasites	73
Giving Birth	79
Internal Parasites	90
Respiratory Infections	101
Serious Diseases	107
Skin Diseases and Disorders	115
Sprains	121
Vitamins and Food Requirements	126

This section explains specific conditions, and offers various modes of treatment.

Broken Bones

For further information, see:

Symptoms	5
Over-the-Counter Medicines	135

Broken bones are defined as fractures, and they affect animals in exactly the same way as humans. They are extremely painful and often debilitating; they should always be attended to as soon as possible.

Basically, there are two types of fractures—simple and compound.* Simple fractures occur when one bone breaks into two pieces but remains inside the animal's skin. Compound fractures occur when the jagged end or ends of broken bone push through the soft tissue and are exposed.

Both types of fracture are almost always caused by some kind of trauma. For example, when animals are hit by cars they often suffer broken bones. Breakage can also occur from being kicked,

*There are many different types of fractures, but for household purposes, simple and compound are adequate groupings.

stepped on, tripped over. There are many causes. Any kind of trauma that can cause a bruise will cause broken bones if the impact is severe enough.

Also, some animals have conditions that may make their bones more prone to fracture. If your pet has rickets or other bone conditions, fractures can be a constant danger. Improper diets and a lack of vitamins may also contribute to bone problems. Animals with tumors or cancer may suffer weakened bones, and as pets grow older, their bones naturally become more brittle and therefore more susceptible to breaking.

Yet, in spite of these hazards and the many causes of fractures, broken bones in animals are generally as uncommon as broken bones in humans. Moreover, while fractures will always require professional attention, they are usually able to be set and corrected.

If your pet has sustained an injury, be alert for signs of broken bones. Animals with fractures will be in great pain and will almost always cry or bite when you touch the injured area or attempt to pick them up. Also, most fractures will in some way immobilize the affected animal. Broken limbs, for example, will not bear weight; broken bones, in general, will often discourage the animal from walking.

In some cases, however, animals will walk on broken bones. The most common example is a fractured pelvis. Dogs (especially the smaller breeds) and cats will occasionally ambulate on this injury when the break is not too severe. Even so, the animal will show extreme distress and will let you know it needs attention.

When fractures are present, the affected area will swell causing the animal to suffer additional pain and discomfort. It is important to chill the injured area in order to prevent this swelling or at least control it. The best method is to apply an ice pack to the fractured part. If an ice pack is unavailable, try using cold, wet compresses. But keep changing the compresses or the area will not stay chilled.

Once you have attended to the swelling, see your veterinarian for professional diagnosis and treatment.

If you are unable to see your veterinarian within several hours after the fracture has been discovered, you should try to protect the injured animal from unnecessary movement. If you can, confine the animal to a small room, like a bathroom. If the injured part is twisted or if it flops loosely (common in broken limbs, forearms, etc.), you can apply a temporary splint to immobilize it. These splints are relatively easy to apply, and almost any material that is firm will be effective in preventing movement.

You can use such things as magazines, thick layers of newspaper, cardboard, or even thick sticks. When using pliable materials like a magazine, wrap it tightly around the injured part and bind it in place by bandaging it with strips of cloth or gauze. If you decide to use nonflexible materials like thick sticks, gently place these sticks on opposite sides of the injured part and bandage as before. But remember, splints like these are only a temporary treatment and professional assistance will still be needed.

Broken bones must be X-rayed to determine the severity of the fracture and the extent of actual bone displacement. After reading the X ray, your veterinarian will treat the break. Fractures are frequently splinted, pinned, or plated, and are sometimes set into casts. Occasionally, veterinarians will even construct special braces or other aids so the animal can function somewhat normally while the fracture is healing. Today, almost any fracture can be treated and corrected. Once the broken bone has been set, the animal's pain will diminish and the swelling should recede.

Questions Most Often Asked about Broken Bones

How can I recognize when my pet is suffering a concussion, and how are concussions in animals treated?

One of the symptoms of concussion can be unevenly dilated eyes. But head injuries in animals are hard to diagnose because several unrelated conditions may produce the same symptoms. For example, tumors, strokes, or any head injury may all cause the affected animal to walk in circles or tilt its head in an unnatural way. Any of these conditions can also cause the animal to vomit, or in severe cases, to go into shock. If your pet does suffer from a concussion, the treatment is complete rest and quiet. Often this entails confining the animal to prevent excess movement.

What about fractured skulls? Can this injury be treated?

Fractured skulls are rarely seen in animals because animals will usually not survive them. If your pet does have this injury, it must be X-rayed to determine the severity. When there is no evidence of brain damage, the animal can be treated and often returns to a normal life.

What about broken jaws? How are they recognized and how are they treated?

If your animal's jaw is broken it will usually be out of normal position. It may hang unevenly or flop loosely. The injured animal will display great pain when you touch its jaw and may not be able to eat or drink. Once diagnosed by a veterinarian, this injury is usually treated by wiring or pinning the jaw bone into a normal position. Affected animals must be kept on soft diets (like baby foods) for several days until the bones start knitting. Then they will be able to eat soft canned foods (like most pet foods). Broken jaws usually heal in three to four weeks. After this condition has been corrected, the pins or wire must be removed by a veterinarian.

What about fractured ribs? How are they recognized and how are they treated?

Animals will sometimes walk with broken ribs, but the area will be extremely painful to your touch and the animal will fight any attempt to pick it up. If the injury is severe—a lot of displacement, animal goes into shock, evidence of internal bleeding like blood in urine—see your veterinarian. Otherwise, the best treatment is time. Broken ribs will usually heal by themselves in two to four weeks.

Do animals ever require surgery as a result of fractures?

Yes, surgery is required when the fracture must be pinned or wired to effect proper healing. Broken hips, for example, almost always require pinning to knit correctly, and veterinarians will sometimes implant artificial joints or bone sockets (in fractured hips) to aid recovery.

Do fractures always require professional assistance to mend correctly?

In most cases, yes. Some fractures (for example broken ribs) can mend without treatment, but even these injuries should be diagnosed by a veterinarian. In general, broken bones should be diagnosed and set by a person who has a good knowledge of anatomy. When fractures are left untreated or are set incorrectly, they may knit unevenly, leaving the animal with a disability. If you suspect your pet is suffering from a fracture, see your veterinarian.

Is there any danger if I delay too long before having my pet's fracture treated by a veterinarian?

Yes. The bone may begin to heal improperly, causing the animal's condition to become more serious. Also, the longer you wait to start treatment, the longer your pet will suffer pain and discomfort.

Do animals ever try to bite or rip their casts off after the fracture has been set?

Unfortunately, yes. This is a common problem. Animals do not understand the purpose of protective casts and often try to remove them. Sometimes animals with fractures can wear special collars that will help prevent this. Confinement also helps because movement will usually increase the animal's discomfort. If your pet's cast does come off, see your veterinarian immediately.

Burns

For further information, see:

Symptoms   7
Over-the-Counter Medicines   137

Even though burns are normally uncommon occurrences, they can strike your pet suddenly and without prior warning. They can happen in or out of doors and they are almost impossible to prevent. Moreover, burns can be debilitating, and they are among the most painful injuries that an animal can sustain. Whenever your pet has suffered a burn, you will want to ease its discomfort as soon as possible.

Fortunately, this injury will cause definite symptoms, and the animal itself will often show obvious distress, alerting you to its condition. Even if you do not witness the injury as it happens, you will quickly recognize your pet's pain and discomfort. Once you have diagnosed your animal's condition, you can begin to treat it. In many cases, treatment can be done at home without professional assistance.

Basically, there are three kinds of burns that can endanger your pet—electrical, thermal, and friction. But only electrical burns will normally be accompanied by the threat of death. However, if thermal and friction burns are left unattended, they can lead to infection and other complications. It is important to treat all burns quickly, before the injury can deteriorate.

Electrical Burns

Electrical burns can be induced whenever an animal comes into contact with flowing electrical currents. Plugged-in appliance cords are an ever present hazard. When pets chew on live cords, they can bite through the protective coating and make contact with the current's path. Fortunately, an animal will rarely do this. If the covering around the wire has worn thin, this compounds the danger. There are other potential causes as well. An improperly insulated appliance can generate this burn, even when the cord that it connects to is fully protected. Another cause of electrical burns is lightning. Pets struck by lightning almost always suffer electrical burns. These burns can damage any part of the animal's body, but the greatest threat is to the heart.

When an animal is jolted by currents of electricity, the resultant shock can stop its heart (cardiac arrest). In many cases, electrical burns are fatal. Sometimes the injured animal will die, even with treatment; even when it survives, there is always the possibility of brain or nerve damage. If your pet is to have any chance at all, you should see your veterinarian immediately. Whether or not you saw the injury happen, the symptoms should be apparent.

The area of the burn will be evidenced by seared flesh and red or irritated skin. In severe cases, the wound may also blister. Pets that live through electrical burns often develop pulmonary edema. They will find it very difficult to breathe, and they may lose color in their mucous membranes (lips, gums, etc.). The animal's complexion can also become pale, or even slightly bluish in color. If your pet exhibits any of these symptoms, you should see your veterinarian immediately. Do not attempt to treat your pet at home. Your dog or cat may need oxygen or other specialized treatment, and you will have to be prompt, or it may not survive.

WARNING When animals sustain an electrical burn, the resulting trauma can send them into shock. This is an extremely dangerous condition, and you will have to treat it even *before* you see your veterinarian. Affected pets will lose color in their lips and other mucous membranes, and their temperatures will begin to fall significantly. Keep your animal warm! Use heating pads or hot water bottles, and cover the pet immediately with a blanket or a heavy jacket. Next, see your veterinarian! Do not delay. Shock is very serious, and the animal should have professional attention as soon as possible.

Thermal Burns Thermal burns are usually caused by household accidents. For example, your pet may be scalded by hot coffee or boiling water. It may inadvertently walk across hot coals. Cats can jump on top of hot stoves, and any animal can be spattered by hot grease. There are many causes, but thermal burns are due mostly to human carelessness. Keep potential sources of danger away from your pet. But even if you exercise caution, an accident may still happen. If your pet is burned, you will recognize the symptoms.

The damage from thermal burns is often visible on the animal's coat. Look for areas of singed or charred fur. If you can see bare skin, it will probably be red or inflamed. If the burn is severe, the skin may also be blistered, or lesions may form. This type of burn can be very painful, and injured pets may show their distress. If you try to touch the burn, your dog or cat may resist by scratching or biting at your hand. Although this injury is not normally fatal, you should begin to treat your pet as soon as possible, before the wound becomes infected. There are several proven methods of home treatment.

The aloe plant (also called the unguentine plant) can be quite effective in the treatment of thermal burns. The thick, jelly-like substance from inside these plants should be smeared on the area of the burn. This will help to subdue the animal's pain and will also temporarily help to reduce the wound's inflammation. This plant can be purchased at many neighborhood plant stores, and it is a good idea to have one on hand.

In addition to the aloe plant, pet-owners can also use Domeboro tablets to treat their animal's burn. This product can be obtained at most pharmacies and is available in both tablet and powder forms. Follow the directions on the product's label to make Burrow's solution, and apply this solution to the area of the burn as a continuous wet dressing. The exact directions and techniques for using both the aloe plant and Domeboro tablets are outlined in "Over-the-Counter Medicines."

Some pet-owners have found Vitamin E oil to be extremely beneficial in the treatment of their animal's burns. This oil can be purchased at many health food stores and is thought to be most effective if it is smoothed on the burn shortly after it occurs.

Thermal burns should improve within several days of household treatment. If the injured region is large or heavily blistered, or if the symptoms of pain and inflammation continue to persist, see your veterinarian.

Friction Burns   Friction burns are generated by a related trauma, usually occuring whenever an animal is forcibly propelled against an abrasive surface. For example, an animal can be struck and dragged by a car or it can slip from an ice patch to rough concrete. There are many potential causes, but friction burns are most often the result of outdoor accidents. This is not a common injury, and it will rarely be fatal when it does happen. Moreover, the symptoms are easy to recognize, and the wound can usually be treated without professional assistance.

Unlike thermal burns, the area of fur around a friction burn will be scraped, torn, or chafed, instead of being singed or charred. The difference will be obvious. In most cases, the wound will display areas of skin that are red, irritated, or rubbed raw. Sometimes there will be accompanying cuts and lacerations,* and eventually scabs may form. Like other burns, this injury can be extremely painful and it should be treated promptly.

*These injuries will have to be treated as separate conditions. Turn to "Common Wounds" for further information.

For the most part, friction burns are treated just like thermal burns. Gently cover the burn with the substance from inside the aloe plant, or use Burrow's solution (from Domeboro tablets or powder) as a continuous wet dressing. If there are foreign particles (pebbles, etc.) embedded in the animal's skin, or if the burn fails to respond to treatment, you should see your veterinarian.

WARNING   Both thermal and friction burns will normally heal with two or three weeks of treatment. However, if the extent and depth of damage to the animal's tissue is unusually severe, it may take longer. In some cases, the burn will need professional attention before it heals. If the burn does not improve within a reasonable period of time, or if any of the symptoms continue to persist, or if the injury becomes infected, see your veterinarian.

Questions Most Often Asked about Burns

How do you treat pets that have suffered a chemical burn, as from acids, turpentine, etc.?

First, wash the chemical agent off of the animal's body with a mild soap and water. Next, try to relieve the pain and inflammation that results from the burn. There are two good ways to do this. You can keep the burn covered with the jelly-like substance from inside the aloe plant, or you can use Domeboro tablets to make Burrow's solution and apply it as a continous wet dressing. If the burn is severe or if the symptoms continue to persist, you should see your veterinarian.

Can I treat my pet at home if it burns one or more of its foot pads?

Yes. As with most burns, you can relieve pain and inflammation by using the substance from inside the aloe plant, or Domeboro tablets to make Burrow's solution. The procedures for applying both of these medications have already been outlined in the Diagnosis and Treatment section of this chapter.* After you have treated the burn, you should bandage it for protection. But if any of your pet's

*See "Thermal Burns."

45   Burns

foot pads are severely burned, do not attempt to treat them at home. See your veterinarian immediately!

Do animals ever suffer severe burns on the insides of their mouths? If so, how are these burns treated?

Yes, they do. Whenever a burn is severe, it needs immediate professional attention. One of the ways that your pet can sustain this burn is by biting through a live electric cord. This can be extremely dangerous, because some animals will die, even with treatment. Do not wait. See your veterinarian as soon as possible!

My pet loves to chew on appliance cords. Is there anything that I can do to discourage this potentially dangerous behavior?

Pets will usually chew on such things as electric cords until they are approximately eighteen months old. During this period, dogs and cats should not be left unattended for any length of time, or they should be confined whenever they are not being watched. Additionally, it is a good idea to unplug all appliances when they are not being used. Of course, proper training and plenty of regular exercise (to prevent boredom) will help your pet to prevent these problems.

My pet has incurred an electrical burn, and it obviously needs oxygen. Can I give it some form of artificial respiration before I bring it to my veterinarian?

Yes. Whenever an animal needs oxygen, you can give it artificial respiration by compressing its chest, releasing the pressure, and repeating the process until it begins to breathe again. If a person in your household has a heart problem, or a severe respiratory condition, you may have access to a small tank of oxygen (obtained from pharmacies). You can use this device to give your pet oxygen while you are transporting it to your veterinarian or an emergency clinic. But remember, whenever you have an emergency, you should call ahead to make sure that your veterinarian (or clinic) can see you when you arrive. You will not want to waste precious time in travel if they cannot see your pet.

If my pet's burn becomes infected, can I treat the infection at home?

Sometimes. If your animal's burn becomes infected, you may be able to treat it at home, but only under professional supervision. See your veterinarian. He or she may have to surgically clean the burned area and remove all dead and destroyed tissue before the infection can be treated.

If my pet suffers a bad burn, will the injury ever induce gangrene, as in humans?

Yes. Whenever a burn is severe, it may eventually produce gangrene. See your veterinarian quickly. All "bad" burns should be professionally treated.

If large patches of fur have been burned off of my pet, will the fur grow back, or do animals scar, like humans?

That will depend on the severity of the burn. If the burn has penetrated all layers of the animal's skin, then the hair follicles will be destroyed and scar tissue will form. Consequently, the fur will not grow back.

Common Wounds

For further information, see:

Symptoms 9

Over-the-Counter Medicines 140

Domestic animals are just as susceptible to cuts and bruises as animals which are not confined.

Even if your pet spends its entire life in the relative safety of your home, it can suffer a wide assortment of wounds.

Dogs and cats can be injured at play, eating, while walking on a leash, or even while they sleep. It can happen anytime, and you should always be prepared to help.

Fortunately, most wounds are not serious and can be treated at home. You can clean and wrap the affected area, ease your animal's pain, and help prevent infection.

Cuts   A simple cut may be caused whenever your pet comes into contact with a sharp object such as glass, razor blades, a knife, or tin cans.

The resultant separation of your animal's tissue will often produce bleeding, but bleeding does not always occur. When bleeding does occur, it must be controlled before you can administer medication or bandage the wound.

This is best done by applying a pressure bandage. Take a clean piece of gauze or cloth and wrap it around some soft padding such as bunched up cloth. Press it gently but firmly against the wound and hold it steady until the bleeding stops.

If an ice bag is available, press it to the affected area. This will work like a pressure bandage and will also help control future swelling.

As a last resort, you can try a tourniquet. But be very careful. If the wound is gushing or continues to bleed after several minutes of treatment, it may need to be sutured. Consult your veterinarian for maximum safety.

Once the bleeding has been controlled, it is important to cleanse the wound before you bandage it. This is done to prevent infection.

Use a cotton pad or swab to apply hydrogen peroxide (medical) or Bactine. You can also wash or soak the wound with agents such as tamed iodine. Make sure you dry the area after it has been cleaned.

Once dry, you should try to have the edges of the cut lying in as normal a position as possible. If the skin is folded or bunched in an abnormal manner, the wound may not heal properly!

Now apply an antiseptic or antibiotic. You can use such agents as furacine, iodine, Merthiolate, or medicated creams. If nothing else is available, use vaseline. Put the medication onto a gauze square or sponge and apply to the wound, while holding the animal tightly.

Next, wrap the gauze square snugly with a gauze roll. You can use a strip of cloth, but it must be clean. Fasten with strips of adhesive tape.

It is important to prevent your animal from removing the bandage. You can do this by extending the wrap into an area which is difficult for the animal to reach. This is where you should fasten it with tape and use enough tape to minimize the chances of slippage or removal.

If your animal does remove the bandage or if it becomes wet, clean and rewrap the wound immediately. Otherwise, change the dressing daily until the cut heals.

Lacerations A laceration is simply a more severe cut. It is usually recognizable by a tearing of the tissue as opposed to a smooth separation. A tear is more prone to swelling and injury to the tissue than a simple cut.

Look for swelling in and around the injured area. Irritation and black-and-blue discoloration of the tissue would also suggest a laceration.

A laceration should be treated in exactly the same manner as a cut. However, the use of an ice bag is now mandatory to reduce swollen areas and prevent future swelling.

Abrasions An abrasion is a spot rubbed bare of skin or mucous membrane and is always caused by some kind of friction. For example, roadburns, rubbing against a rope, and even licking with the animal's own tongue can result in an abrasion.

Look for redness, swelling, and heat.

Once you are certain that your pet suffers from an abrasion, you can ease its discomfort through a soothing application. Use an agent such as Solarcaine, Nupercainol, Unguentine ointment, Vaseline and sulfur, a medicated cream, or calamine lotion.

Apply the medication with your fingers or by using a cotton or gauze pad. Make sure that you spread it liberally over the affected area.

You do not have to bandage the wound, but your pet must be prevented from licking off the medication.

Apply the medication as needed to ease irritation and accelerate healing.

Bruises and Contusions

A bruise or contusion is an injury without any cuts or lacerations and is the result of impact.

Bruising may occur whenever your animal is struck by a ball, stick, or car, or when it runs into a stationary object such as a tree. Falling objects such as books or ash trays can also produce painful bumps and contusions.

Usually a bruise or contusion can be recognized by black-and-blue discolorations in surrounding tissue.

Treat your pet with cold applications or ice bags. If you administer these directly after impact, you can often reduce or even prevent swelling.

Serious Wounds

In general, any wound that does not heal after several days of treatment may require professional attention.

If your animal's cut or laceration is gushing blood or if bleeding will not stop, it may indicate damage to an artery or a main vein. *Consult your veterinarian immediately!*

If your animal has suffered a severe bruise, it may go into shock. This is especially common after being struck by a moving vehicle.

Shock will often signify internal bleeding, and you should respond with immediate action. Your animal is in shock when its mucous membranes (such as lips and gums) turn pale and when its body temperature begins to drop significantly.

Keep your pet warm! Use a heating pad or hot water bottles and cover it with a blanket or heavy jacket.

Shock is *extremely serious!* Consult your veterinarian *as soon as possible!*

Questions
Most Often
Asked about
Common
Wounds

If my pet suffers a cut or laceration, what are the chances of infection?

If you treat the wound immediately, you minimize the chances of infection. Even so, the wound may still become infected.

How can I recognize infection in my animal's cut or laceration?

If the wound becomes red and swollen, it is probably infected. Consult your veterinarian.

If my pet suffers a cut on the bottom of its paw, how should I treat it?

Cuts on the foot pad heal extremely well. Treat it as you would a normal cut or laceration. The bandage should be wrapped like a cast, completely covering the foot, and extended well up the limb. You must keep it dry and prevent your animal from removing it.

If my pet suffers a cut or laceration on its face, is it more difficult to treat?

Yes. This area almost always heals better if sutured; but do not delay. If you wait too long before you see your veterinarian, it will be much more difficult to suture properly.

How can I tell if my animal's cut or laceration needs to be sutured?

If the skin around the injured area is bunched or retracting, or if it has slid back, exposing other tissues, the wound almost always needs suturing.

Is it possible for my animal to be allergic to any particular disinfectant or cleansing solution?

Animals do not suffer allergies as often as humans. They can, however, exhibit sensitivity to a specific medicine or lotion. If this is the case, simply substitute another medication to serve the same purpose.

If my pet suffers a severe bruise or contusion, should I change its diet during the recovery period?

No. Continue to feed it well-balanced meals. Make sure that fresh water is easily accessible.

How can I tell if my animal is suffering great pain from a bruise or contusion?

Touch the damaged area. Your pet will cry, wince, bite, or struggle to get away if experiencing severe pain. When your pet holds up a limb or refuses to put weight on it, it is also a sign of pain. Also, some animals will hide when experiencing great pain. This is especially true with cats, who are far less willing to tolerate our "interference" than dogs.

What can I do to ease my animal's pain?

You can give your dog aspirin if it does not upset its stomach. Turn to "Over-the-Counter Medicines" for correct amount and frequency of dosage.

However, *never* give a cat aspirin. There is not much you can do to ease your cat's pain except make sure it is warm and comfortable.

If your animal's pain is persistent, it may suggest a fracture. Consult your veterinarian.

Constipation

For further information, see:

Symptoms   11

Over-the-Counter Medicines   143

Constipation is one of the more common disorders that can affect your dog or cat. By definition, it means infrequent or difficult evacuation with retention of feces. While it can cause your pet a great deal of discomfort, constipation is rarely serious if treated quickly. The first step is to recognize its presence.

The only sure method of diagnosing constipation is to observe your pet during a bowel movement. If your animal strains repeatedly without passing stool, it is probably constipated.

Dog owners can detect this condition in its earliest stages, either by watching their pets during regular walks, or by periodic examination of their animals in designated toilet areas. Cat owners, however, will have a much harder time for two reasons: Litter boxes are often secreted in out-of-the-way locations, and cats cover their stools with litter almost immediately after passing it. Even then, most cat owners can be aware of a difference in the consistency of their pet's stool when they change their cat's litter. This can be the first sign of constipation.

If your dog or cat avoids food, it may be constipated. Another indication can be a change in personality. If your pet is unusually nervous or irritable, check its toilet area for a recent stool. If you think your cat is constipated, watch it in the litter box to be certain. But if your cat is male, make sure he is attempting a bowel movement. If he struggles while trying unsuccessfully to urinate, he may suffer from a condition much more dangerous than constipation, and you should see your veterinarian immediately.

Unfortunately, treating constipation is much easier than preventing it. There are many causes. Young animals,* for example, can develop constipation from chewing on bones, sticks, toys, furniture, and various other objects. If even a small amount of foreign material is ingested, it can impact in your pet's digestive system and hinder the passage of waste material, often causing constipation.

Grown-up pets may not chew as much, but they will swallow almost anything. Dogs are the worst culprits. They are always mouthing loose objects and will occasionally swallow one. The result is usually an obstructed digestive system and constipation. Veterinarians report such unseemly items as panties, stockings, anklets, and even steel ball-bearings being passed in a dog's stool.

Nature is another cause of constipation. As animals mature, their digestive systems can become sluggish, often causing chronic constipation problems. In older males, this condition can result from an enlarged prostate gland that slows down the movement of material in the large bowel. This causes the material to dry and harden, often forming into a large, unpassable mass which results in constipation.

*In very young puppies and kittens, constipation is a rare occurrence. This condition may signify a more serious ailment and you should consult your veterinarian.

If this condition occurs repeatedly, your male pet can develop serious problems. Frequent straining coupled with an enlarged prostate can cause the tissue on the sides and underneath the anus to break down with a resulting hernia (perineal hernia). If your mature, male pet is often constipated and seems to be in pain during normal activities, it may be herniated. Consult your veterinarian for diagnosis and treatment.

Even your animal's diet can be the cause of its constipation. Many low-residue foods such as organ meats (liver, kidney, etc.) can produce a congealed, pasty stool that is hard to pass. On the other hand, necessary ingredients like bulk and fibers can help to regulate your animal's bowels.

In fact, there are many foods that will help prevent constipation. By properly controlling your pet's diet, you can aid its digestive system in breaking down food for rebuilding cells and eliminating waste. Feed your pet regular portions of brans, cereal foods, and assorted vegetables such as peas, carrots, and corn. Hard foods such as kibble are also effective in preventing constipation.

Many cat owners feel that milk will also prevent or ease their animal's constipation. This is simply not true. While milk is indeed a laxative, it usually causes diarrhea in mature cats and will not generally help when constipation is present.

If (and in spite of your best efforts) your animal becomes constipated, you should begin to treat it as soon as possible.

In simple constipation, an infant-sized glycerine suppository or a suppository of soap is usually sufficient. Enemas will also work, if you can convince your pet to hold still while you apply them.

In some cases a stool softener can be the best cure. You may want to visit your local pharmacy and purchase a container of Meta-Mucil, an excellent softener. Give your pet just a pinch (mixed with food) at every meal and taper off as your animal's condition improves.

Other treatments are mineral oil and milk of magnesia. Instructions for administration and correct dosage of these are given in the "Over-the-Counter Medicines" section on constipation.

*If my dog or cat is constipated, will it hide from
humans as a symptom of its condition?*

Some animals when impacted or in distress will hide from their owners, choosing to suffer in solitude. Others will hug their owners, demanding an unusual amount of attention. This is their way of telling you when something is wrong and needs treatment. If you know your animal when it is normal, you will be able to recognize when its behavior is abnormal, indicating a condition that needs to be corrected.

*I have two cats and they share the same litter
box. How can I tell if one of them is constipated?*

In the early stages it will be very difficult to know if one of your cats is constipated. But as your cat's condition gets worse, it will become more obvious. For example, the constipated cat will not eat as much and will probably become irritable or lethargic. If your cat's bowel is impacted, it may vomit after attempting to eat.

*I don't have time to watch my cat go in and out of
the litter box. Is there any other way to confirm
the presence of constipation?*

Unfortunately, no. You can rely on secondary symptoms, such as avoiding food, and eventually your cat will display signs of not feeling well, but a concerned owner will watch his cat in the litter box before starting treatment for constipation.

*If my constipated dog has become more irritable
than normal, are my children in danger of being
bitten while playing with it?*

The average dog will not bite anyone just because it is constipated. But it may resent being played with or picked up, especially if its digestive system is painfully impacted.

If my dog repeatedly shows little enthusiasm for its regular walk, can I assume it suffers from constipation?

Not necessarily. Your dog could be suffering any of several physical conditions and may even fear his walk for emotional reasons. For example, he could have been recently frightened by firecrackers or other loud noises or even by another animal on a previous walk. Check for secondary symptoms and determine if he is straining during a bowel movement before beginning treatment for constipation.

If I am treating my dog or cat for constipation, and it is not really constipated, can any of the various medications be harmful?

None of the treatments for constipation will severely harm your animal if it is not constipated. However, if you have misread the symptoms, your pet may be suffering from a much more dangerous condition such as inflammation of the bladder. If your pet is eating normally, and still shows signs of constipation after two or three days of treatment, consult your veterinarian immediately.

What are the more serious complications that prolonged constipation can lead to? Can my pet actually die from constipation?

Yes, severe impaction will eventually kill your animal if it is not corrected. The most serious complication is loss of body fluid or dehydration. When an animal is dehydrated, it will have great difficulty in swallowing. Cats will dehydrate faster than dogs. However, you will certainly see signs of extreme ill health before your animal dies, and unless you are neglecting your pet's health, you should have ample opportunity to see your veterinarian.

How can I tell if my animal is dehydrated?

One way to detect dehydration is by placing your finger inside your pet's mouth. If the area you touch is dry and sticky, your animal is probably dehydrated. There is another method that is also reliable. Pick up an area of your pet's skin by holding it between your thumb and forefinger. Stretch it as far as possible and then let it go. If it is slow in returning to a normal position, it usually indicates dehydration. The slower it returns, the more your animal is dehydrated. If it is very slow, see your veterianarian immediately.

Dental Care

For further information, see:

Symptoms   12

Over-the-Counter Medicines   145

While dogs and cats do not develop cavities like humans, they can still suffer from dental problems such as bad teeth and gums. Sometimes these problems are due to owner neglect, but other conditions can also affect an animal's teeth.

The biggest reason for bad teeth in animals is accumulation of food and tartar deposits. Diseases like gingivitis and uremia also contribute to dental problems, and so do some infections that affect the mouth and throat. Other problems can arise from pieces of foreign materials that impact between the animal's upper teeth. Even soft diets can lead to bad teeth. Most of these conditions, however, will produce similar symptoms so you can usually recognize when your pet needs attention.

In some cases you will be able to see tartar deposits or particles of food or hair that have accumulated on the animal's teeth. You may even be able to see bits of foreign material that have wedged between the upper teeth (across the roof of the mouth). If the problem is being caused by a mouth or throat infection, the animal may cough or discharge substance from its nose or mouth. All of these symptoms are usually accompanied by bad breath. Diseases like gingivitis and uremia will also produce specific symptoms.

Gingivitis is a disease that often evolves from encrusted teeth and large amounts of accumulated tartar. This condition will inflame your animal's gums and loosen its teeth. Ultimately, the animal's teeth will either fall out or need to be extracted.

An organic disease such as uremia can also affect your pet's teeth. This condition originates in the animal's kidneys and usually results in uncomfortable dental problems. The affected animal can display large deposits of blackish tartar on its teeth and will usually have extremely bad breath. The animal will also have a constant thirst and may drink excessively for relief.

Unfortunately, organic diseases and infections of the mouth and throat cannot generally be prevented. If any of these conditions are causing your pet's dental problems, you will need to seek professional assistance before they can be corrected. But with a little care, you can usually protect your pet from many of the common problems that may affect its teeth and gums. Often, this entails little more than a regular cleaning of the animal's teeth.

Animals can go for a relatively long period of time (compared to humans) without needing their teeth cleaned, but tartar will eventually begin to gather at the gum line. If the tartar remains, it can lead to conditions like gingivitis, causing the animal's gums to recede. Fortunately, encrusted teeth and gingivitis can usually be prevented through the proper dental care.

Try to clean your pet's teeth at least once each month and more if needed. If the tartar is noticeable, attempt to scrape it off with your fingernail. Next, mix 1 teaspoonful of salt or medical hydrogen peroxide into ½ cup of tap water and apply the solution to your animal's teeth with a cotton swab or a soft toothbrush. Now brush thoroughly, massaging your pet's gums as well as its teeth.

Regular cleaning can also help to dislodge collected materials and eliminate bad breath. If you initiate these procedures while your pet is still young, it will learn not to be resistant when you handle its mouth.

If you forget to clean your animal's teeth, the tartar may accumulate to dangerous levels, and you will be unable to scrape it off. Do not let this happen or you will need professional assistance to clean the teeth. Your veterinarian will normally have to anesthetize the animal to gain access to all of its teeth. In some cases, the tartar will be removed by special ultrasonic devices. This is a time-consuming and bothersome process for both the animal and the owner.

Besides regular cleaning and tartar control, there are other ways to protect and strengthen your animal's teeth. For example, allow your pet to chew on acceptable objects, and make sure that some kind of hard food (like kibble) is included in its regular diet. These methods of prevention will require little effort and pay great dividends. Once again, you should begin to guide your pet's chewing habits while the animal is still young.

Puppies and kittens usually develop permanent teeth at approximately five months of age. As the teeth push through the surface, the area inside the animal's mouth becomes naturally irritated and uncomfortable. Chewing relieves this irritation so make sure your puppy or kitten has its own objects on which to teethe.

Young dogs should be furnished with an old slipper or shoe or various toys like strips of rawhide or hard rubber bones. These toys can be purchased at your pet store and most supermarkets, and they will usually keep your pup from chewing on valuable furniture and other personal items. If your pet chews one of its objects into fragments, you should remove it quickly. The loose bits will almost always be swallowed, and this can cause your pet to suffer diarrhea or constipation, or even a more serious condition.

Young cats should also have designated objects to chew on. The action of their chewing eases the pressure on the gums as the milk teeth are forced out. The teething may also cause frequent drooling and, in some cases, can even cause the kitten to suffer a great amount of teething pain. If your pet is in obvious distress, or if during this critical period it vomits and avoids food, you should consult your veterinarian. Once again, you should replace all objects that become fragmented.

After your pet has grown through the teething stage, you should begin to introduce some kind of hard food into its regular diet. Additionally, you should continue to allow it to chew on acceptable objects.

Hard foods (like kibble) will rub against your animal's teeth as it chews them up into digestible pieces. This rubbing will automatically prevent tartar from forming on your animal's teeth. Dogs will also benefit from chewing on raw marrow bones and cats can help to strengthen their teeth with raw chicken necks. Both of these food items are easily obtainable at your butcher shop.

When young dogs are first given raw marrow bones, they tend to play with them instead of chewing on them. But as the young animal continues to play with the bones, it will learn to suck out the marrow. This is the best way to prevent excess tarter. The chewing action will push the bone's hard external surface against the teeth and scrape off any food remains. This action will also massage the animal's gums.

But make sure the bones you give your dog to chew on are raw, and not cooked. Cooked bones become soft and are easier for dogs to crack and swallow. If your dog does ingest bone chips, they can become impacted in its digestive system. This can cause the animal to vomit or suffer pain, and you may have to see your veterinarian before the condition can be corrected. Some dogs will even fragment and swallow raw bones. If your pet cannot handle bones, give it something else to chew on.

Kittens should be started with pieces of raw chicken neck. You can buy a whole neck and then cleave it into manageable segments, making sure that no piece is small enough to be easily swallowed. Next, freeze these pieces for easy storage. Then once a week, let a piece thaw and give it to your pet. As your cat develops, increase the amount of chicken neck until it is big enough to handle the whole bone. Adult cats (especially indoor pets) may ignore the chicken necks if they have not grown accustomed to them at an early age. If you continue to persevere, they may finally eat it. Chicken necks are the best and easiest way of maintaining good dental health in your cat. Of course, both dogs and cats should not be allowed to have bones that have been chewed into fragments and slivers that they can swallow.

In addition to bones, your dog or cat should continue to be given its own objects to chew on. Whenever an animal chews on hard surfaces, the teeth are automatically cleaned and often strengthened. Chewing can also provide good benefits for the animal's gums. In regard to dental problems, preventative care is absolutely the best cure.

If the worst does happen, and your pet loses all its teeth, the animal will still survive. In fact, dogs and cats can live quite comfortably without their teeth. The affected animal must be limited to semimoist or soft meals, but many pets (even with teeth) prefer these foods. Toothless dogs often appreciate Gaines Burgers or Top Choice, and even most canned foods will still be edible. Toothless cats will usually respond to Tender Vittles, or even soft baby food meats, as well as most canned foods.

Questions Most Often Asked about Dental Care

Can animals ever chip or break teeth by chewing on extremely hard objects?

This is certainly possible, but if the animal's teeth are normally healthy, it would have to be considered a freak accident. Dogs and cats have stronger teeth than humans, and they will rarely be damaged during the chewing process.

What procedure should I follow if my dog or cat does chip or break a tooth?

In most cases, animals can chip or break teeth without needing special care. Veterinarians often find broken or even severely chipped teeth when they examine the mouths of household pets. If your pet has recently damaged a tooth, you should not necessarily rush to seek professional assistance. Consult your veterinarian only if the affected animal is in obvious discomfort or pain.

Can animals ever be fitted with bridges or false teeth?

A few dogs and cats have been fitted with false teeth, but this procedure is expensive and is not normally done. Dogs and cats do not need their teeth in order to survive and can live quite comfortably without them.

Do animals ever suffer toothaches like humans do? If so, what are the symptoms?

Probably, yes. It is difficult to give an exact answer because animals do not show pain in the same way as humans. In some cases, dogs and cats with loose teeth will chew on one side of their mouths or they may even avoid food completely. If your pet exhibits one of these symptoms, you should see your veterinarian.

Do dogs and cats ever develop dental problems from eating overly sweet foods, like humans?

No. Animals do not usually develop cavities like their human owners. Even if your pet has a "sweet tooth," the adverse effects (if any) of the sugar will be eradicated by the scraping action of chewing on hard foods, like kibble. Make sure your pet has some form of hard food included in its regular diet two or three times a week and the animal's teeth will generally remain healthy and clean.

If foreign materials have wedged or impacted between my animal's teeth, should I use dental floss to try and remove them?

No. Most animals will not sit quietly while you attempt to use dental floss on them. But you should attempt to remove these materials before they can harden into tartar. In some cases, the material will be on your pet's tooth and you should scrape it off with your fingernail. If it is wedged between the animal's teeth, use a cotton swab or a soft toothbrush to remove it. If it is impacted between the animal's upper teeth, pry it out with a pliable object like a toothpick or your fingernail. Do not use rigid objects like a pin because the animal may resist and suffer an unnecessary injury as the result. If any of the foreign materials cannot be removed, you should see your veterinarian for further diagnosis and treatment.

Should I ever use toothpaste or toothpowder to clean my animal's teeth?

An animal's teeth do not need to be brushed with agents like toothpaste in order to be cleaned. While pastes and powders will not do any harm, they are unnecessary and messy. Even if your pet holds still during the application, you will have trouble rinsing the toothpaste from its mouth. If the paste or powder foams during rinsing it can spill over the animal's mouth, creating a messy condition in its fur.

What are some of the hard foods that can clean my pet's teeth?

Dogs will benefit from foods like kibble, milk bones, and various dog biscuits. Cats can be given any of the dry cat foods that are available in your supermarket. Of course, the best cleaners are raw marrow bones for dogs and raw chicken necks for cats. Your pet should be given some kind of hard food about two or three times a week. If you give your pet hard food every day, make sure it is given as a treat and not left around for your pet to chew on throughout the entire day.

Diarrhea

For further information, see:

Symptoms   14

Over-the-Counter Medicines   146

Simple diarrhea can be extremely bothersome to your dog or cat, but much of the time it can be treated and corrected right at home.

Simply defined, diarrhea is an abnormal frequency and liquidity of fecal discharge. There may be any number of factors which induce this condition, but the result is almost always a painful inflammation of the bowels which can cause your pet great discomfort.

If your animal has diarrhea, avoid all laxative or irritating foods. Remove milk, oils, and other greasy items from your pet's menu immediately! Stay away from high fibers such as bran and any bulk foods such as kibble or dry catmeal. These foods will only irritate the swollen areas within your animal's system.

Dog owners have a special problem. Some canned dog foods have a high fat content. If ingested, they will only aggravate your dog's condition. Unfortunately, nothing on the can's label will tell you if the contents are too fatty. You have to open the can and look at the contents. The container should be opened the same way in which it was stored, not "upside down." If there's a relatively thick layer of fat on top, feed your dog something else until the illness is over.

If you have time, prepare equal parts of cooked hamburger and boiled rice. Make sure that you drain all excess grease from the hamburger. This is also a good recipe for cats but they may not cooperate by eating it.

In fact, your cat may resent any change from its normal diet—but that diet may be the sole cause of the diarrhea! When this is the case, the diet must be changed before you can effect a cure. For example, many people believe that cats thrive on milk and fish. But for most cats, exactly the opposite is true.

An adult cat will usually develop moderate to severe diarrhea when given milk, so milk must be avoided. As for fish, cats in general seem to crave it, but too much of a good thing can produce ill effects. If you are feeding your cat fish more than three times a week, it may be a contributing factor to its diarrhea. Over a long period ·of time your pet could even develop certain vitamin deficiencies from eating too much fish. However, the remedy is quite easy. Vary your cat's menu and you'll help prevent diarrhea!

In fact, most diarrhea can be prevented if some precaution is taken. Here are some of the common causes of diarrhea and what you can do to eliminate them.

The most common of all causes is teething. Young animals, especially puppies, are constantly chewing on foreign objects such as brooms, toys, match sticks, foil, shoes, and almost anything else they can bite on.

While this is good for their teeth, all too often the end result is diarrhea. (The objects that they chew on may carry germs or bacteria that can be introduced into their systems before the young animals have developed tolerance.)

Even if your pet is already through the teething stage, ingesting chemical irritants such as detergents, soaps, and motor oils are always a sign of danger.

Ice-melting compounds are also hazardous. Any animal that steps in one may later lick its feet and swallow some of the substance, often causing vomiting, and sometimes diarrhea.

Even plant leaves can occasionally cause diarrhea.

Obviously, you can't monitor your animal's actions a hundred percent of the time. But if you clear its environment of irritating and infectious objects, you can reduce the chance of diarrhea!

When your animal is teething, keep it in a closely confined area such as a medium-sized room. Remove anything that you consider to be a potential source of illness, and make sure you provide proper teething material to chew on.

If your adult animal has the "run of the house," make sure that chemical irritants are safely out of reach. If you have plants, never spray them with a chemical solution unless you're absolutely sure it's safe! And never buy a plant which is considered poisonous.

But no matter how safe you try to be, your pet may still contract diarrhea. You can usually correct this condition by giving your animal small doses of Pepto Bismol or Kaopectate. Turn to "Over-the-Counter Medicines" to check correct amounts and time schedules.

If the diarrhea persists after twenty-four hours, or if there's any evidence of blood in the stool, consult your veterinarian. This may signify internal bleeding or a more serious infection.

If your dog continues to have diarrhea without any sign of blood, it may suggest parasites such as hookworms or whipworms.

Any of the more serious conditions can usually be corrected with little or no difficulty. But act quickly, and consult your veterinarian!

*If my pet has diarrhea, can I continue to feed it
table scraps?*

Absolutely not. Dry foods such as dog meal are also out.

*I have two cats, one has diarrhea and the other
doesn't. Should they have separate litter?*

This is always advisable. Diarrhea can be infectious and it's better
to be safe.

*Can my animal get diarrhea from being exposed
to the stool of another animal that has it?*

Unfortunately, there is always the possibility of infection. Usually,
it's spread through the cause rather than the symptom of diarrhea.

*If my pet has diarrhea can I catch anything? Can
my child?*

Not from the diarrhea itself. Again, this would depend on the
cause. But even so, the chances are so infinitesimal that for all
practical purposes the answer is no.

Do gas and diarrhea usually come on together?

No. Gas is not normally associated with diarrhea, and it can usually
be cleared up by altering the diet.

*My pet seems to have diarrhea one day and then
the next day it doesn't. Then it does again. What
does this indicate?*

Intermittent diarrhea can mean your pet is having trouble from
parasites. Consult your veterinarian.

*My animal has diarrhea and its stool is a funny
color, almost pitch black. Could this be a sign of
something more serious?*

Yes. This can indicate internal bleeding. Consult your veterinarian.

Will diarrhea change my animal's disposition?

Not usually. If it does, it may be a sign of severe pain.

*Can diarrhea ever be caused by a human disease,
for example, influenza?*

Almost never. Animals and humans share very few common diseases.

External Parasites

For further information, see:
Symptoms   15
Over-the-Counter Medicines   148
NOTE: See "Skin Diseases and Disorders" for
additional material on external parasites.

External parasites are unhealthy and unclean. They attach themselves to an animal's body and feed off it, often causing related skin disorders with uncomfortable symptoms like itching and scratching. Sometimes they can even affect humans. Fortunately, however, some of these parasites can be recognized and treated without the assistance of your veterinarian.

For example, the most common kinds of external parasites are fleas, ticks, and lice. They can be seen on your animal's body and are easily eliminated.

The less common types of external parasites (with the exception of maggots) are invisible to the human eye and will need professional diagnosis and treatment from your veterinarian. None of these parasites can be treated at home. Besides maggots, this group includes sarcoptic, demodectic, and ear mites.

Fleas Dogs and cats suffer more from fleas than any other external parasite. Your pet can be susceptible whenever it goes outside. Fleas are especially plentiful in the country, in grassy areas, and areas with loose or sandy soils. But fleas also inhabit the cities and no area is completely immune. Your pet can even catch fleas from close contact with an affected animal. When your pet is infested, it will display noticeable symptoms and the parasites themselves are easy to detect.

Fleas are small, brown bugs that often move rapidly through their victim's coat. If your dog or cat is affected, this movement can sometimes irritate its skin, causing your pet to bite or scratch at the infested area. This increases the chance that your pet will develop related skin problems like hair loss or scabs.

But when fleas stop moving, they may cause other problems. After settling on your animal's body, they will bite through the skin and ingest its blood. As your pet is bitten, the flea deposits a toxin on its skin. Many animals are allergic to this toxin and may develop flea-bite dermatitis or other skin conditions as a result of contact.

After fleas have ingested and digested your animal's blood, they will deposit black waste matter on its coat. These unsightly flea droppings look like commas and periods. Also, fleas will sometimes lay their eggs inside your animal's coat. If you see evidence of either flea droppings or eggs, brush your pet's fur thoroughly and begin to treat its condition.

Fleas are controlled by the use of flea collars and medallions. You can also use any of the flea sprays, powders, baths, or dips that are available in your pet store. But it is important that you read the directions on the label. If you are a cat owner, make sure it reads "for use on cats" before you use it on your pet.

If your animal has fleas, they may also infest your premises. Be sure to spray the surrounding furniture and carpet when you de-flea your pet, otherwise you may be bitten when walking through your home. If you are not treating your pet with a spray, you should obtain one designed for this purpose from your veterinarian or pet store.

Ticks   Ticks are small, round, dark bugs with hard external shells. They are usually found in wooded areas, and they will affect dogs more often than cats. When an animal comes in contact with ticks, they fasten onto the animal's body and suck its blood. Like all external parasites, ticks may cause symptoms and conditions of the skin. They can be detected by looking carefully through your pet's fur. Once discovered, they should be eliminated as soon as possible.

The best way to remove ticks is to just pull them off. This usually results in a harmless bruise on your pet's body that will recede in two or three weeks. Additionally, you should use one of the commercial tick powders, sprays, dips, or baths because you may be unable to see all of your animal's ticks. Once again, you should treat your premises to prevent or control infestation.

Lice   Lice are small, dark, grey bugs that do not appear to move on your animal's body. About twenty years ago they were a common problem, but today they are less common and do not warrant much discussion. They can be eliminated by the same powders used for fleas and ticks.

Maggots   Maggots are also rare. These parasites are a larval form of blow flies that lay their eggs in open wounds, urine-soaked fur, or areas of skin that are moist from constant licking. If your animal has lesions, keep them clean and dry and there will usually be no problem.

Maggots can sometimes be found in your animal's stool, especially if it is picked up infrequently. They can also be seen in litter boxes that are not kept clean. Unfortunately, your animal's maggots cannot be treated at home. This is a serious problem and if your pet is affected, you should see your veterinarian at once.

Mites Sarcoptic, demodectic, and ear mites are external parasites that are invisible to the naked eye. They can cause various skin disorders and related symptoms. It is almost impossible to determine whether or not your pet has mites, because you can often relieve or temporarily correct the accompanying skin problems. If you are treating your dog or cat for a skin condition that recedes and reappears, it may suffer from mites and you should visit your veterinarian.

If your dog* has mange, for example, it may appear to be suffering from dry, dandruffy skin. By treating your animal for dry skin, you may relieve the symptoms, but the condition will continue to resurface. Eventually, you will need professional assistance.

There are two types of mange in dogs, and both are caused by sarcoptic or demodectic mites. While mange if fairly common, it can only be diagnosed by a skin scraping and microscopic examination. So see your veterinarian.

Ear mites are parasites that live and thrive in the ears of dogs and cats. These mites are usually spread through contact with other animals that have them. They will cause your pet to intensely scratch its ears or the area around its ears.

If your animal is affected, the skin inside its ears will be dry and inflamed, exhibiting varying amounts of dry, brown wax. As the mites continue to irritate the mucous membrane of the ear, the ear will produce increased amounts of wax and cerumen in self-defense.

These parasites must be killed before your pet's condition can be corrected. Afterwards, the animal's ears must be routinely cleaned to remove wax and other debris that can cause secondary infection. If you suspect your pet has ear mites, you should consult your veterinarian.

*Mange is a disease that almost never occurs in cats.

*Will the use of flea collars and medallions really
prevent my pet from getting fleas?*

Unfortunately, no. They will certainly help, but even if you take
the most stringent precautions, your dog or cat will still be susceptible to this common parasite.

*When I bathe my dog, should I use a flea
treatment as a preventative?*

Absolutely not. You should use flea treatments only when your
animal is infested. Remember, all of the flea medications are
necessarily toxic in order to kill the fleas. If one of these agents is
used excessively, the poison may eventually kill your dog.

What causes lice in animals?

Your dog or cat can get lice only through close contact with an
already affected animal or by living or playing in an area where an
affected animal has been.

*One of my pets has mange. Are my other pets in
danger of catching it?*

Yes, mange is highly contagious. This disease is almost always
passed from one animal to another. If one of your pets is affected
(and the condition has been confirmed by your veterinarian), be
sure to confine it and have all of the animals in your household
examined as soon as possible.

*If my dog or cat has mange, can I be affected?
Can my children?*

Yes, sarcoptic mange can sometimes be caught by humans. However, this form of mange is self-limiting and can be easily eliminated by treating the affected animal. Once your pet has been
treated, and you are no longer exposed to the disease, it will disappear by itself.

Can ear mites be prevented by routinely cleaning my animal's ears, and what is the best method of cleaning them?

Ear mites are passed through contact with an affected animal, and there is no way to completely prevent them. After your animal's ear mites have been eliminated by your veterinarian, you should clean its ears to remove excess wax and relieve its discomfort. If the area inside your pet's ears is moist, insert a cotton swab and gently clean the affected ear. If the area is dry, or if you can see wax deposits, apply several drops of mineral oil* with an eyedropper and let it settle for fifteen or twenty minutes. Then gently remove the wax with a cotton swab. Repeat daily until your animal's condition improves and then decrease the frequency of cleaning until the condition has been eliminated.

*Mineral oil is extremely bland and will not hurt your pet's ears or its eyes.

Giving Birth

For further information, see:

Symptoms   17

Over-the-Counter Medicines   150

Giving birth can be an important event in the lives of female pets and their owners. But the world of dogs and cats is already over-populated, so owners should exercise some thought before allowing their pets to reproduce. If you are willing to accept the responsibility of caring for new animals and eventually finding them good homes, then your pet's pregnancy and ultimate delivery can be a rewarding and educational experience for both you and your family.

Animals reproduce out of a need to propagate the species, and during certain periods, they can mate indiscriminately with members of their own species. Female dogs will develop the urge to reproduce approximately twice a year, but female cats can be irregular. The female's body will generate an odor that attracts males and the process of mating begins. This period of mating is called heat, and it is only during heat the animals can become pregnant.

After conception, the gestation period for both dogs and cats is sixty to sixty-three days or about nine weeks. During gestation, the animal will display an increasingly swelled stomach and her breasts will develop to maturity. Most pregnancies are relatively trouble-free, but animal owners should be prepared to help their pets whenever such help is needed. To do this, owners should be somewhat knowledgeable in all phases of animal reproduction—the precautionary period before heat, the pregnancy (gestation), the delivery, and the first few days of new life.

Before Heat   Most pet owners tend to love their animals, and they usually want their female dogs and cats to have "just one litter." But reproduction in animals is not "fulfillment," as it is for many female humans, and owners should consider all of the ramifications before allowing their female pets to reproduce.

The pet world is already overcrowded, and each year veterinarians must destroy hundreds of thousands of young animals that are not adopted into human homes. Owners should secure good homes for their animal's litter before the animal is mated. Even so, puppies and kittens are not usually ready to leave their mothers until they are six to eight weeks old. Owners must be willing to devote time, energy, and some expense to bringing their animals through the first few weeks of life. This is especially true in the case of puppies, who normally remain with their mothers for eight weeks before they mature enough to move into new homes.

If you are willing to accept all the responsibilities of bringing new animals into the world, you should see your veterinarian before allowing your pet to mate. Female pets should be examined, vaccinated, and tested for intestinal parasites* prior to mating. If you are unwilling to bear the responsibility for new animals, you should make sure your female pet is spayed to prevent unwanted mating.†

*When female pets are infested with intestinal parasites during pregnancy, they often pass these parasites to their feti while the unborn litter is still being carried.

†It is also advantageous for pet owners to have their male animals altered. This procedure is discussed in the special chapter entitled "Basic Pet Care."

Female dogs and cats (bitches and queens) should usually be spayed while they are still young. Except for brood bitches, it is preferable to spay them after one heat period and before they reach two years of age. When animals are spayed young, they rarely develop breast tumors and never contract uterine infection (pyometra). These conditions are fairly common in older, unspayed bitches and queens.

Sometimes animals are not spayed because the owner plans to breed them, or has bred them. But once the breeding is finished, the animal should be spayed.

Heat   Female animals will usually start to come into heat at six months of age, with a few starting earlier, and others starting later. Thereafter, the animal will go in and out of heat at varying intervals throughout her life. This interval can vary greatly in cats, but female dogs will generally be affected about every six months. Both dogs and cats display specific symptoms while in heat, and rural dog owners can sometimes see an indication even before their bitch comes into heat.

When a bitch is about to start her cycle, the change within her system will produce an odor that makes her attractive to males. In the country, male dogs are usually free and on the loose, and they may start to visit the premises of the female in anticipation. These visits can begin up to two weeks before the bitch actually comes into heat. But in the city, dogs are usually confined or on leash, and this harbinger will not normally exist. City dwellers will have to rely on the visible symptoms that are present from the first day of heat.

When a bitch is in heat, her vulva will swell and she will release a bloody discharge from it. The first day of heat is considered to be the first day of bleeding, and dogs generally remain in heat for about three weeks. But dog owners will not always notice when this discharge begins. If the quantity of blood is small, the bitch may clean it off herself before the blood is seen. Some dogs will go through their entire cycles without allowing any blood to remain visible, and their owners will have to be alert to spot it.

Even though the heat period is normally three weeks long, dogs may actually be fertile for only a few days. Usually this fertility is achieved during the middle of heat, from the tenth to the fourteenth day. But there can be a wide variation among bitches and the days they will mate. You must control your dog throughout the entire heat period to prevent mismating.

When cats are in heat, they will often be restless and unhappy. They may cry, meow, or roll a lot. They can eat poorly and may urinate outside the litter box. Some queens will even tread with their hind legs while pointing their rear ends upward, in the air. People who have not previously seen a cat in heat, may believe the animal to be sick, or in pain. They may even consult with their veterinarian, only to learn that their pet is fine. These are the normal indications of a queen's cycle, and there will rarely be a need for professional assistance.

Compared to dogs, cats have a very short cycle. Dogs can be in heat for more than twenty days, but a cat's cycle will seldom remain for longer than seven days. During this period the cat can be mated. Put your queen with a tom and observe its actions. If the queen does not mate, you should try again during the next heat period. It is important for unspayed female cats to mate; otherwise, they may begin to develop an uncomfortable condition called cystic ovaries.

Cats do not ovulate unless they mate, and without ovulation, they cannot complete their cycles. Uncompleted cycles will eventually lead to more frequent periods of heat. Consequently, a high percentage of unspayed cats will be in heat more and more frequently, usually developing cystic ovaries as a result. This troublesome problem will make your cat miserable, so if your queen is a household pet, it becomes even more important to have her spayed.

Pregnancy (The Gestation Period)

After your bitch or queen has mated, the pregnancy or gestation period will begin. The first day of gestation is considered to be the date of conception, and the final day is the date of delivery, or whelping. During this period, the animal will usually behave somewhat normally, requiring only a minimum of extra attention from the owner. In fact, most of your help will either be precautionary, or in preparation for the whelping.

There are two precautionary measures that are easy and important to take: First, you should consult with your veterinarian well in advance of the expected date of whelping. Second, you should control your animal's diet.

Your veterinarian should be able to answer your questions, and will tell you generally what to expect, especially if this is "your" first litter. Additionally, you should know what procedure to follow if your veterinarian is unavailable when the birth occurs. He or she will refer you to a colleague or the closest animal hospital in case you need quick help. Your veterinarian can also instruct you in regard to your pet's diet.

It is important to feed your animal nutritious and well-balanced meals throughout her pregnancy. Vitamin deficiencies and poor diets can lead to conditions that will sometimes affect the unborn puppies and kittens. Look at the label on your pet's canned food. You will be able to see if the product is enriched in some way with vitamins and minerals. If it is, it will be beneficial to your pregnant pet. Any of the major brands will generally provide a good meal, and many dry foods are also fortified with vitamins and minerals.

But good diets are even more effective when combined with a supplement of vitamins and minerals. These supplements can be obtained at your pet store or from your veterinarian, and you should follow the instructions on the product's label.

After attending to your pet's nutrition, you can begin to prepare for the whelping. Both dogs and cats should be provided with whelping boxes at least three or four weeks prior to the anticipated date of delivery. The animals will need time to grow accustomed to the box, and they should even be encouraged to sleep in it.

The basic box can be a cardboard container, or an empty suitcase, and in the case of dogs, it should be large enough for the mother to stretch out. Cat owners, however, should use containers that are big enough for both the mother and her kittens. Next, you should make the container a comfortable place to be in.

Place the box in an area of your premises that the animal is at ease in, and line the bottom of the box with plastic or linoleum to prevent the seepage of any liquids. But your pet may not want to lie against these linings, so prepare a bed (inside the container) by using soft cloth towels or newspapers. Cat owners can also use light flannel blankets. Finally, show the box to your dog or cat and encourage her to use it.

As the animal gets closer to whelping, her belly will get larger and larger. Her breasts will continue to develop until shortly before the day of delivery. Approximately twenty-four hours before whelping, bitches will start to nest by scratching, tearing newspapers, and performing other digging actions, and their temperatures will drop by about one degree.

If you live in the country, it is important to control your dog or cat during the final hours of pregnancy. Do not allow her to be out alone, because some animals will attempt to sneak off and deliver their litters in seclusion. Most births are generally trouble-free, but if there is a problem during whelping, you will want to be present to provide assistance.

Whelping

In the ultimate moments of pregnancy, the birthing process will begin to operate inside the animal's body. The bitch or queen will suddenly become very quiet. This quiet usually signifies the beginning stages of labor, and the animal is probably experiencing her first contractions.

The mother will continue to contract (at increasingly frequent intervals) until she enters into the final phase of labor; then she will begin to have bearing-down contractions. Arching her back, she will draw her legs up underneath herself and begin to push hard. If everything is normal, you will soon see a bulging between the vulva and the anus. As the animal continues to strain, the vulva will part and the membrane that is protecting her baby will begin to protrude. At this point, the new puppy or kitten will usually just slide out. If the birth is more difficult, the mother will strain and push for a longer period of time before she delivers her baby.

If your animal starts to contract and all at once becomes still and motionless, or if she continues to strain during the last part of labor without producing her baby, the animal is in trouble and needs *immediate* attention. Call your veterinarian! Sometimes the delivery itself will be hampered by an abnormal presentation of the baby, and you will also need professional help.

Newly born animals should emerge from the vulva head first or bottom first, and the head or tail should always be accompanied by the front or rear feet. If only the baby's head or tail is visible, the mother and her baby can be in danger, and you should make *prompt* contact with your veterinarian!

Sometimes the presentation can be completely normal (head with front feet, etc.), but the baby will stop moving when it is only part way out of the vulva. Grasp the baby's body lightly with your hands and slowly rotate it back and forth over an arc of approximately 180 degrees, or about one half of a circle. As you are turning it, gently (very gently) begin to pull the baby out of the mother's vulva. If the baby does not come out easily, or in a very short time, you need *immediate* help from your veterinarian!

Sometimes both the presentation and the delivery will be normal, but the baby will emerge still encased in its protective membrane, or placenta. While you cannot prevent this problem from happening, you should be prepared to offer help in case it is needed.

Careful owners will put a pair of scissors, thread, rubbing alcohol, and a bowl or deep plate within easy access before the babies are born. When the animal enters into labor, some of the alcohol should be poured into the bowl and a few long pieces of thread should be cut from the spool and soaked in it. If the birth is normal, you will not need these items. But if the baby is still inside the membrane, you will have to act fast.

Cut the placenta with the scissors and make sure that the baby's nose is out of the fluid. Young animals must breathe by themselves as soon as they are born, and it is essential that you make sure they are exposed to the air. Once you have prevented a possible suffocation, you will have to tie and cut the umbilical cord before removing the animal from the placenta.

The placenta will be attached to the baby's umbilicus and it will have to be tied off before it can be cut free. Grasp this membrane about ¾ of an inch from the baby's body and tie it tightly with a piece of thread that has been disinfected in the alcohol. Now it is safe to sever the placenta. Be sure to cut it on the side of the tie *away* from the baby's body and begin to work the baby free of the membrane. The entire procedure, from cutting the placenta open to tying and cutting the umbilical cord, should be done carefully and quickly. It is important to get the baby out of danger as soon as possible, and you should be ready to repeat the process if it becomes necessary.

Bitches and queens almost always have more than one baby, and an abnormality that affects the birth of one young animal may affect other members of the same litter. While some animals will emerge trapped in their protective placentas, this is not a common occurrence; however, in rare instances, this problem can endanger the entire litter. Be sure to disinfect several pieces of thread in the rubbing alcohol before the mother begins to deliver her babies.

The First Few Days of New Life — Newly born animals should begin to breathe and move immediately after emerging from the mother's vulva. After the baby has been born, the mother will usually nuzzle and lick it in order to clean off the remains of the protective membrane. If for any reason, the mother cannot or will not clean the baby, you should do it for her. Use soft cloth towels and wipe the puppy or kitten briskly until it is clean and dry. Once the mother has delivered her entire litter, you should observe her babies, making sure that they begin to nurse.

It is very important for young animals to nurse on the mother's first milk, or colostrum. Besides providing strength and nourishment, this milk will contain antibodies for diseases to which the mother is already immune. Babies that do not nurse will become weak and eventually they may die. If one of the babies has been pushed off to the side, or appears (for whatever reason) to be unable to eat, you should put it near one of the mother's breasts and encourage it to start nursing as soon as possible. If any of the babies are still not nursing after several hours, you should consult your veterinarian.

Puppies and kittens are normally born with their eyes and ears closed, and this should not cause you any concern. The eyes and ears will usually open by themselves within the seventh to tenth day of life. If they remain shut after the baby is two weeks old, however, there may be a problem and you should make contact with your veterinarian. If you want to remove your puppy's tail or dew claws, it should be done three to five days after the animal is born.

Puppies and kittens will continue to nurse until they can survive on their own. When they are eight to twelve weeks old, they should be examined and vaccinated.

A Common Myth Regarding the Birth Cycle

Some people believe that a nursing mother cannot come into heat, but it is not uncommon for cats to come into heat and even mate while they are still nursing their litters. Dogs, however, have a longer interval between heat periods and will normally not come into heat for approximately four months after they have given birth.

Questions Most Often Asked about Giving Birth

When my pet is in heat, will it ever endanger or attack my children?

No. The basic personality of an animal does not change during heat. Some pets may become more nervous, especially if they are confined; if your animal is not normally dangerous to humans, it will not be dangerous when it goes into heat.

Do female pets always have periods of heat? If
not, what causes this condition, and what can be
done to treat it?

In some cases, an animal may never go into heat. This usually
indicates that their ovaries have not matured. Although your veterinarian might be able to correct this condition (with hormones),
it is generally better to have the animal spayed—unless of course,
it is valuable for breeding.

If a bitch or queen is frightened or upset during
gestation, are they likely to have a miscarriage?

No, this is very rare. In normal pregnancies it takes extreme
circumstances to produce an abortion.

How long must I wait after whelping before my
animal will allow me to handle her offspring?

If your dog or cat is normally friendly and affectionate, then her
newly born animals can be handled immediately. But it is best to
leave them alone if the whelping process was normal. In some
cases, weaker offspring may need to be placed at or near a nipple
to ensure that they get colostrum for nourishment and antibodies.

Do female pets ever attack or try to kill their
offspring after whelping? If so, what can the
owner do to prevent this?

Unfortunately, some mothers will kill or even eat their young after
whelping. All bitches and queens should be supervised both during
the whelping process and after it. If they attempt to injure their
young, then you should separate the mother from her offspring. In
these cases, you will probably have to hand-rear the newly born
animals if they are to survive.

If there are other animals on the premises, will
they ever try to harm a mother's newly born
puppies or kittens?

Sometimes, but not always. Both male and female animals may try to attack strange young; some males may even try to mother the newly born animals. This can be very distressing to the mother, and she may become very protective. You can prevent this by isolating the mother and her offspring from other animals in the household. Mothers with newborn are usually apprehensive, and they may not even allow people to come near them unless they are very familiar. You should be especially careful if there are children on your premises.

Do female dogs and cats ever suffer from menopause, like humans?

No, not as a rule. As female animals grow older, their heat periods may become shorter, and the intervals between their heat periods may be longer, but in many cases, the animal will not be affected.

Are bitches and queens likely to become sterile in their old age?

Sometimes, but not necessarily. In older bitches the heat period will usually cease or come at longer intervals. But even so, they can still be fertile, and if they do go into heat, they will still have to be watched or confined.

Do animals ever suffer from hereditary conditions like humans?

Yes. Animals have genes, just like people, and physical characteristics can definitely be inherited. For example, purebred animals often produce progeny that look like the parents. Unfortunately, bad conditions like congenital hip dysplasia* can also be inherited.

*Congenital hip dysplasia is a condition that causes a very poor formation of the animal's hip joint.

Internal Parasites

For further information, see:
Symptoms 19
Over-the-Counter Medicines 151

Internal parasites live and flourish inside the bodies of dogs and cats. They can seriously weaken an animal's defenses, and in some cases, they can even be fatal. If your pet is inhabited, it will suffer from uncomfortable symptoms like diarrhea and vomiting; certain kinds of infestation can even produce convulsions or pneumonia. For all of these reasons, internal parasites should be attended to and eliminated as soon as possible.

Unfortunately, these parasites are usually difficult to diagnose and treat at home, and improper treatment can endanger your animal as much or more than the parasite itself. If you believe your pet to be infested, you should seek professional assistance.

There are several different kinds of internal parasites, but tapeworms and roundworms are the most common culprits. Both of these worms can be seen in the affected animal's stool. If left untreated, these parasites can be quite harmful to your dog or cat, but they will rarely be fatal.

Hookworms, whipworms, and heartworms are found less frequently than tape and roundworms, but they can be more dangerous to your pet. Coccidia are also less common, but they are not as threatening. Toxoplasmosis affects mostly cats and is relatively uncommon, but the parasite that causes this disease can endanger humans.

None of these parasites can be seen by the human eye, and they produce symptoms that are not necessarily obvious. Symptoms like diarrhea and vomiting, for example, are often treated as separate conditions while the actual cause (the parasite) remains unchecked inside the animal's body. Because these internal pests are "invisible," pet-owners can misdiagnose parasitic conditions for long periods of time, allowing them to further deteriorate their animal's health. Unfortunately, it is this group of internal parasites that can be the most dangerous to your pet. If the condition continues to be neglected, the infested animal may even die. Check the "Symptoms" section carefully. It is important to consult your veterinarian at the first suspicion of trouble.

All of the internal parasites should be diagnosed by a microscopic examination of the host animal's stool or by other specialized laboratory tests such as blood tests. You should obtain a professional confirmation even if you can see the parasite, as in the case of tapeworms or roundworms. Animals sometimes harbor more than one type of internal parasite, and it is always best to be safe. Do not neglect your pet's condition; make contact with your veterinarian.

Once the problem has been isolated, you can begin to treat the specific parasite(s) that is threatening your pet. While there are several commercial products that are available in your pet store, you should only use them with your veterinarian's guidance. An improper medication or dosage can kill your pet, so rely on your veterinarian. Much of the time you will need to use a special prescription that is stronger, safer, or more effective than any of the various commercial products. In most cases these parasites can be controlled and eliminated, and your pet will rapidly return to good health.

Tapeworms

Tapeworms are unwanted tenants that can inhabit the bodies of either dogs or cats. They grow and thrive by robbing needed nutriments from their victim's digestive system, and while they are usually not fatal, they can be quite destructive and should be eliminated as soon as possible. Unfortunately, they can only be prevented by sequestering your pet indoors, and even this method is not 100 percent effective.

Tapeworms are usually spread outdoors, and they are more prevalent in the country than in the city. Essentially, there are two modes of contamination. First, animals can become infested by swallowing fleas that carry the eggs of unborn tapeworms. After these fleas have been ingested, the eggs will develop in the aniaml's body. Second, animals can become contaminated by eating certain kinds of wildlife (rabbits, squirrels, etc.) that are already infested. Once the old host has been digested, the tapeworm will begin to function inside the body of the unlucky animal that ate it.

After they have secured a host, these parasites will begin to pillage nourishment from it. They do this by firmly fastening themselves to the animal's intestinal wall and draining nutrients before they can be put back into the animal's system. As they continue to feed, they gradually increase in size, adding segmented portions that stream through the intestinal folds of their host. The larger they grow, the more nourishment they need in order to survive. These parasites can develop into lengths of one to two feet in cats, and even longer in dogs, depending on their size. It is even possible for your pet to support several tapeworms at the same time. Fortunately, these parasites always signal their presence, and there are effective treatments to kill them.

As tapeworms grow, worm-part fragments will break off from the mother worm and pass through the affected animal in its feces.

These worm pieces will be readily visible in the animal's stool, and may also be seen under the host's tail, around its anus, or in its regular sleeping place. Once you spot the evidence, you should make contact with your veterinarian. Do not attempt to treat these parasites without a professional consultation. Your veterinarian will first confirm the problem, and then oversee the necessary steps to eliminate it.

Roundworms (Ascarids)

Even though roundworms are sometimes called "puppy worms," they are the parasitic enemy most often found in cats. In general, puppies and kittens are more susceptible to this worm than older animals, and they can even be born with roundworms if their mother was infested during pregnancy. This parasite will invade the host's intestine; it lives by withdrawing proteins and minerals from the animal's alimentary system. Severe infestations can travel to the animal's lungs, sometimes causing pneumonia, which in turn can cause the animal's death.

Roundworms are common all over North America, and like tapeworms, they are usually spread outdoors. Unlike tapeworms, they are mostly spread through the feces of already infested animals. These feces are usually laced with thick-shelled eggs that remain potent for a long time. When unsuspecting animals step in the affected stool, the eggs can become dried on their feet. Later, when the animal licks itself, the eggs can be ingested, ultimately causing roundworms to develop inside its body. While these parasites can be picked up anywhere, the most common areas of contamination are the places where animals congregate, such as parks and fields. Outside of deworming females before they mate, roundworms are difficult to prevent. But you should always be able to detect their presence, and there are several medicines that will terminate their existence.

If your pet is infested, these parasites will be visible in its stool. Look for cylindrical, spindle-shaped worms with slightly pointed ends. They will appear to be yellowish white in color, and they are usually two to four inches long. If the infestation is severe, other symptoms may develop.

Ordinarily, roundworms will not cause serious problems in mature, well-nourished pets. But if the condition is left untreated, the worms can cause the pet to suffer from diarrhea and cramps. In some cases, the parasite can even induce convulsions. If you believe that your dog or cat has roundworms, you should consult your veterinarian before the condition becomes severe. After the parasite has been confirmed, he or she will prescribe a suitable treatment.

Hookworms Hookworms are named for the tiny hooklets that extend from their bodies. They attach these hooks to the walls of their victim's intestines, and then they feed from tissue juices and the blood of the animal's bowels. While hookworms appear in dogs of all ages, they are only occasionally found in cats. Like roundworms, this parasite is usually spread through contaminated feces, but the hookworm larva is more apt to thrive in warm weather climates and in moist and sandy soils. The southern and Gulf states are the major hookworm regions. However, hookworms are now becoming common in more northern areas.

In addition to licking off affected feces, there are other ways this larva can enter your pet. For example, the larva can infiltrate through open cuts, or an animal can play with (chew on) objects that were previously contaminated. Even prenatal infestation is possible.* Some dogs are unusually susceptible to hookworms and often develop chronic conditions, whereas other dogs in the same household may never have them. Hookworms cannot usually be prevented, and while some symptoms may indicate their presence, others will be confusing and indefinite, making hookworm very hard to spot.

In infested puppies, hookworm disease may resemble canine distemper (see "Common Diseases") or it may not. Like distemper, it can also be fatal. Mature pets can develop an inflammation of the bowels, resulting in varying degrees of diarrhea, often

---

*Although rare in cats, the hookworm may invade the feline embryo and have a devestating effect on newborn kittens. Look for severe weight loss, fever, coughing, discharges, and listlessness. You should see your veterinarian immediately, or the kitten will probably not survive.

with blood in it. But some animals will exhibit no symptoms at all. The infested host can become listless or even anemic, but not always. Some animals will continue to appear normal and behave in a normal manner. Unlike tapeworms and roundworms, hookworms cannot generally be seen in the animal's stool. Whenever you believe this parasite to be inside your pet, you should consult your veterinarian. But you will not always know when hookworms are a problem. In fact, there is only one sure method for catching these parasitic thieves.

Owners should have a semiannual examination made of their pet's stool. Fortunately, most animals can carry hookworms for a long period of time before the infestation becomes serious. A six-month stool check will usually catch them before the condition becomes acute. This examination will also be beneficial in controlling the other internal parasites that can harm your pet. Once your veterinarian discerns the problem, he or she can begin to treat it. Do not attempt to treat hookworms at home. If your dog appears to have a chronic condition, your veterinarian will supply you with a preventative medicine. Most of the time these parasites can be easily eliminated and your pet will return to good health.

Whipworms
Like hookworms, whipworms will affect dogs rather than cats, and the parasite is usually spread through contaminated feces. Whipworms are slender and coiled, and they can exist all over North America. They are present within an animal's colon and cecum* and will slowly drain the host's vitality. If left untreated, they can seriously endanger your pet's health and will sometimes even cause its death. So it is important to consult your veterinarian at the first signs of infestation.

The general symptoms can be loss of weight, vomiting, and bloody diarrhea. In advanced cases, the diarrhea is more severe and is often accompanied by painful cramps. In time, the host can become dehydrated and may even die. These worms cannot be seen by the human eye, so you will have to rely on a professional analysis of

*The cecum is a pouch at the juncture of the small and large intestine, somewhat approximating the human appendix.

your animal's stool. After the whipworm has been detected, the treatment and elimination process can begin. But you should never attempt to treat these dangerous parasites at home.

Because of the inaccessibility of an animal's cecum, whipworms used to be difficult to eliminate. In many cases, the normal method of treatment was surgery; but this procedure was expensive and not without the risk of serious complications. Today, however, there are several new and highly effective worming remedies that will control and kill the whipworm, and surgery is no longer necessary.

Heartworms

Heartworms can infest either dogs or cats, but they are generally uncommon in cats. This sometimes deadly parasite will attach itself to the right side of an animal's heart or in its pulmonary arteries. Once in place, they will begin to reproduce. Ultimately, there can be several hundred of these worms adhering to the host's heart and artery surfaces. When their number is sufficiently large, they will begin to infest other body organs like the host's kidneys and its eyes. They are probably the most dangerous of all internal parasites. Unchecked, the heartworm will make your pet miserable and will eventually kill it.

At first, these parasites were found principally in the Gulf and Atlantic Coastal states, but now they are common throughout the United States and Canada. Heartworms are always spread through the bite of contaminated mosquitos, causing infestation to be prevalent in late spring and summer. This parasite will generally produce specific symptoms, and you should be aware of what they are.

Heartworms can cause the host to tire quickly, and in advanced cases, the animal may become extremely listless and lethargic. Dogs will cough and pant excessively, even in cold weather. As the infestation progresses, the affected animal can lose weight, develop diarrhea, and exhibit an unhealthy coat. If any of these signs are evident, you should speak to your veterinarian. Whenever these symptoms are being caused by heartworms, your pet will always need professional help.

Heartworms are almost always confirmed through a blood test, but in some cases, an X ray must be taken of the animal's heart. Dogs should have their blood tested each spring prior to the mosquito season, whether or not these parasites are suspected. If the test proves negative, your veterinarian will probably prescribe a daily dose of preventative medicine. You should continue to administer this medicine up to two months after the mosquito season has ended. And if the blood test proves positive, the parasites should be eliminated professionally. You should never attempt to treat your animal's condition at home.

Coccidia Coccidia are one-celled parasites that live in the bowels of dogs and cats. They are not as common as other internal parasites, and they are usually less dangerous to the host. When they do strike, they are more apt to infest puppies and kittens than older and more mature pets. Kittens are especially susceptible after weaning. While coccidia are found less often than worms, they can contaminate the pet in a variety of ways.

Young animals can be very susceptible during their tenures at pet shops. They can sometimes become infested from teething on or swallowing contaminated objects. Older pets can swallow coccidia-laden flies or eat contaminated poultry (mostly true in cats.) Since the symptoms of this parasite are not usually severe, they can be easy to overlook.

Affected animals may show weakness and develop diarrhea. They can also lose weight. In advanced cases, the animal may run a fever and display a discharge from its eyes and nose. While coccidia are not normally fatal, you should still consult your veterinarian when the signs are evident. This relatively innocuous parasite produces many of the same symptoms as the more dangerous worms. To ensure your pet's health, you should have professional diagnosis and treatment. If the parasites are indeed coccidia, they will be ferreted out by a stool analysis, and your veterinarian will oversee their extinction.

Toxoplasmosis

Toxoplasmosis is a parasitic infestation that affects mostly cats. It is spread through the feces of already affected cats and by the eating of raw meats and other raw foods that are contaminated. Unfortunately, this parasite produces no symptoms at all. It is usually discovered accidentally, by a veterinarian performing stool or blood tests for the purpose of detecting other conditions. But once toxoplasmosis has been diagnosed, your veterinarian will be able to eliminate it easily. This condition is not normally fatal (or even very serious) in cats, but the real danger is to humans.

Pregnant women, for example, are especially susceptible to this parasite. If there is an expectant mother in the same household with an infested cat, precautionary steps are necessary. Some other member of the household should clean the litter box, and it should be cleaned frequently. The feces should be flushed down the toilet, the box itself should be rinsed with ammonia (and allowed to dry) before filling it with new litter. The cat should be fed foods that have been canned, cooked, or frozen. Do not feed your cat raw foods. Like cats, humans can also become infested by eating raw meats or raw eggs, or by drinking raw milk, if they are contaminated with the parasite.

Common Myths about Internal Parasites

There are two commonly held beliefs regarding internal parasites that are simply not true. First, many people think that animals can get worms from ingesting milk or sugar; and second, that when an animal slides (or drags) its rear end on the ground, it is infested with worms. Neither of these suppositions has any basis in fact. Although feeding your pet milk or sugar can be disruptive to its digestive system, it will never bring on worms; animals that slide on their bottoms are almost always in discomfort from obstructed glands.

Dogs and cats have oval sacs (or glands) that are normally emptied by pressure when a formed stool discharges through their anus. These glands have narrow ducts that can plug up easily, especially in smaller animals. When this happens, the animal will generally suffer from itching and discomfort. Affected pets may seek relief by dragging or sliding their bottoms on the floor. If the ducts do not open, the glands will continue to swell and may even abcess.

Fortunately, you can treat your pet at home. Hold a warm, wet compress against the animal's anus, and repeat the treatment two or three times a day until the condition improves. If the dragging or sliding becomes unusually severe, or if the condition persists after a few days of treatment, you should consult your veterinarian.

*My pet has diarrhea. How long should I continue
to treat this condition, before having my pet
checked for internal parasites?*

If there is blood in the diarrhea, you should see your veterinarian as soon as possible. Otherwise, you can attempt to treat the condition at home. But if the diarrhea persists after twenty-four hours of treatment, you should consult your veterinarian. Unless your pet has recently had a stool analysis, your veterinarian will probably want to do one, to check for internal parasites.

*If an animal is infested with internal parasites,
is it likely to scratch or bite at its skin out of
discomfort?*

An infested animal will rarely do this. There may be a few cases when hookworm larvae will cause skin irritation, but these cases are the exception rather than the rule. If your pet is biting or scratching at its skin, this action is probably being caused by another condition.

*Do internal parasites ever affect an animal's
teeth or bones?*

Not directly. But if the animal is not well nourished and if it also suffers from chronic diarrhea, then it may develop certain nutritional disorders that can affect its bones.

Can internal parasites ever cause an animal to
suffer from brain damage?

This is possible, but it is also extremely unlikely. It can happen only if the parasite or its larval form becomes lodged in the animal's brain.

Can the stress caused by internal parasites
induce my pet to suffer from a stroke or a heart
attack?

Not really. In some cases, heartworms will cause changes in the animal's circulation, and this may result in heart disease. But this would only be likely to happen in chronic cases of heartworm, and even so, the animal will not usually suffer from a heart attack or a stroke.

I have two pets. If one of them is suffering from
internal parasites, is the other one likely to
become infested?

Possibly. Whenever one of your pets has internal parasites, you should have all of the animals on your premises checked for the same condition. Take a stool sample from each of your pets and give these to your veterinarian for analysis.

Once my pet's condition has been diagnosed as
an infestation of internal parasites, how long
will it take to eliminate them?

Worming programs can vary greatly, but two worming sessions, spaced approximately three weeks apart, will usually be sufficient to eliminate most of these parasites.

Respiratory Infections

For further information, see:
Symptoms   22
Over-the-Counter Medicines   153

Animals are not usually affected by the colds, flus, and other respiratory infections that are contagious in humans. But respiratory problems are quite common in animals, and they can range from mild to very severe. Your pet can suffer from a virus that is normally nondangerous, like laryngitis, or a virus that may be fatal, like distemper in dogs.

Many of these conditions are caused by bacterial infections. Others may result from allergies. Still others can be secondary conditions resulting from various viruses. There are many causes.

Your animal's respiratory infection can be temporary or chronic. Some of these conditions are contagious in animals and others are not. But most of these conditions will produce similar symptoms, and mild infections will usually improve within several days.

If your dog or cat exhibits symptoms like sneezing, coughing, or running eyes, it probably suffers from a respiratory problem. But if the animal remains bright-eyed, active, and continues to eat normally, the condition is usually not serious and it is safe to wait several days to see if it improves. However, if your pet becomes lethargic and loses its appetite, or if you can see a purulent (pus) discharge from its nose, the condition may be more serious and you should see your veterinarian.

Besides general conditions, your pet may suffer from specific conditions like tonsillitis, laryngitis, rhinitis, sinusitis, etc. Any of these problems may really be secondary conditions that have developed from other viruses.

In tonsillitis and laryngitis the affected animal may be hampered by swollen glands and this condition can cause difficulty in swallowing. Laryngitis will also alter the sound of your pet's voice. Infections like rhinitis and sinusitis can inflame your animal's nasal passages which often results in labored breathing. These conditions are rarely serious and should improve quickly. If any of these infections persist, however, or if the animal's symptoms are unusually severe, you should consult your veterinarian. In some cases, the animal will need to be treated with antibiotics before the condition can be corrected.

Allergies, asthma, and sinus conditions are generally chronic and hard to correct. While animals are not usually as allergic to food items as humans, they do suffer from allergies. This condition can be caused by bee stings, and affected animals may display related skin conditions such as hives. Allergies can also cause congestion which will impair breathing. If you suspect your pet is suffering from an allergy, you should see your veterinarian. In some cases, your pet will need to be looked at by a specialist in allergies, and your veterinarian will refer you to another doctor.

If your dog or cat has asthma, it will usually have great difficulty in breathing and may wheeze repeatedly while struggling for air. Some asthmas are allergic in nature and are more common when pollens are high and when plants and leaves are dry, such as in the autumn. This condition is almost impossible to cure completely.

Your veterinarian may be able to treat your pet's discomfort and ease its breathing, but the asthma will probably continue to reappear throughout the animal's life.

If your pet is suffering from a sinus condition, it may be heavily congested. Additionally, your animal can snort or discharge a purulent substance from its nose. These conditions are generally chronic and often develop from more serious respiratory infections. Once again, your veterinarian may be able to relieve your animal's symptoms, but will probably be unable to effect a permanent cure.

There are many other kinds of respiratory problems that can affect your dog or cat. For example, there are various nonspecific viruses that may or may not be contagious in animals. In general, there is little you can do to protect your pet from respiratory infection, but there are some precautions that can be taken.

When the weather is cold and wet, be sure to dry your pet whenever it comes in from outside. If you have a short-haired dog, it will probably benefit from wearing a coat while out in inclement weather. But even if you are very careful, your pet may still have respiratory problems. In some cases, you will be able to treat the symptoms at home.

If your animal is heavily congested, it may be relieved by more moisture in the air. Try using a vaporizer or a humidifier. If your vaporizer has a special place for medications, insert a small amount of Vick's VapoRub. Dogs can also benefit from certain medications.

For example, you can give your dog aspirin to temporarily relieve minor aches and pains. If your dog has a sinus condition, you can use commercial products like Sinutab; and you can even treat your dog's cold or cough with human medicines. See "Over-the-Counter Medicines" for correct dosage and frequency of application.*

*The instructions for giving aspirin to dogs are outlined in "Over-the-Counter Medicines" for "Common Wounds" and "Broken Bones."

In some cases of respiratory infection your pet may be extremely lethargic and obviously very sick. Take its temperature. If the fever is over 102 degrees, you should see your veterinarian as soon as possible. These symptoms can be indicative of dangerous diseases that may prove fatal even with treatment. Cats, for example, can suffer from calici virus and rhinotracheitis. Dogs can be endangered from distemper (often accompanied by pneumonia) and parainfluenza, sometimes called kennel cough (see "Serious Diseases" for further information).

These conditions are highly contagious in animals, but for the most part, they can be prevented by proper inoculation. Make sure your pet is vaccinated about once a year and there will be little danger from these diseases.

Questions Most Often Asked about Respiratory Infections

Do dogs and cats ever get colds like humans?

Yes, they do. Animals (like humans) will sometimes suffer from colds and mild cases of sniffles. These conditions may display symptoms similar to colds in humans, but supposedly they are not caused by the same viruses.

Do dogs and cats ever need their tonsils taken out like humans?

Yes, but only in very rare cases. Twenty or thirty years ago, it was quite fashionable for dog owners to have their animal's tonsils taken out at the first sign of tonsillitis. But today, especially with the advent of antibiotics, this operation is almost always unnecessary.

Can my animal's respiratory condition be treated by administering large doses of vitamin C?

It is uncertain whether or not this treatment will actually correct or relieve your pet's condition. Few veterinarians will ever recommend this treatment, but some animal owners have tried it on their own, with mixed results.

*Are respiratory problems more likely to affect
animals in the winter than in other seasons?*

Not really, but when the weather is cold or damp, you should be
willing to take normal precautions. For example, make sure your
dog or cat has a well-balanced diet and feed it at least once a day.
Also, if you own a short-haired pet, the animal should not be left
outside in cold weather for any length of time unless well protected
by a coat or sweater. Depending on how cold the weather is, even a
coat or sweater may be inadequate protection if the animal is left
outside for a relatively long period of time.

*My pet is suffering from a respiratory problem.
Does it need to be kept warm, as is common in
humans?*

If your dog or cat has a respiratory condition, it will generally be
sufficient to keep the animal out of drafts. If your house is very
cold, however, you may want to cover the animal with some kind of
protective covering, like a blanket. Otherwise, your pet's hair will
normally keep it warm.

*Will being "caught in the rain" affect otherwise
healthy dogs and cats? Will it make them more
susceptible to respiratory conditions?*

The answers to these questions can depend on how long the animal
was exposed to the inclement weather and the severity of the
storm. For the most part, however, animals that can come inside
to a warm house will not be overly affected. In rare cases, especially if the animal is not well-nourished, it can develop a serious
condition like pneumonia. If your pet begins to shiver repeatedly
after being out in a rain storm, and if the animal is obviously very
sick, you should see your veterinarian.

Are most viruses contagious in animals?

Yes, but some conditions are more highly contagious than others;
and some animals are especially susceptible to these viruses and

others are not. Upper respiratory conditions are usually the most contagious in animals, and in some cases, they can also be the most dangerous. Fortunately, most of the conditions that may be fatal, like calici virus in cats and distemper in dogs, can be prevented with inoculation. Make sure your pet receives the proper shots approximately once a year.

If my pet is suffering from a respiratory infection, will it have generally lowered resistance to other nonrelated conditions?

Yes, any sickness will tend to lower the body's resistance, and this is true in both animals and humans. But if your pet's condition is mild, or if the animal is being properly cared for and is eating, then the body's defenses will not usually be hampered enough to cause a problem. However, if your pet is suffering a severe respiratory condition, or if the animal is lethargic and avoids food, you should see your veterinarian quickly.

Serious Diseases

For further information, see:

Symptoms 24
Over-the-Counter Medicines 156

A disease is defined as a definite morbid process, having a characteristic train of symptoms. It can affect the whole body, or any of its parts. Additionally, its etiology, pathology, and prognosis may be known or unknown. Some of the diseases that affect animals can be extremely serious, because they can be fatal, with or without treatment.

While there are several conditions that are considered dangerous to pets, some affect only dogs, and others can only be caught by cats. Rabies will affect either dogs or cats. All of these conditions will generally cause recognizable symptoms, but by the time you spot them, it may be too late to help.

In some cases, the particular illness may have no effective treatment, so the animal will have to be destroyed. In other cases, treatment will not ensure a return to health. This is why protective vaccination is so important. Prevention is always the best cure, and each of these conditions can almost always be prevented. See your veterinarian. If you do not have your pet inoculated against the dangerous diseases that can kill it, you may be solely responsible for its death. Here are the serious diseases that can affect your dog or cat if it has not had the proper vaccinations.

Dogs There are four extremely serious diseases that are peculiar to dogs. They are canine distemper, infectious canine hepatitis, leptospirosis, and infectious canine tracheobronchitis. *Fortunately, these diseases can usually be prevented by a yearly vaccination, either with individual vaccinations or in combination.* Protect your pet! Make sure that it is regularly vaccinated. If your dog dies from one of these diseases, you may have only yourself to blame.

Canine Distemper Canine distemper is a dangerous disease that can affect your dog's central nervous system. It is an extremely complex condition that is caused by an airborne virus; it is spread through direct or indirect transmission, making it highly contagious. It is usually fatal, and even when the dog recovers, it can be left with chronic twitching, partial paralysis, and brain damage. If your dog is to have any chance at all, you will have to diagnose this condition as soon as possible.

The most commonly occurring symptom is acute diarrhea, but there are other indications, too. The dog can run a fever, cough, and display a purulent discharge from its eyes and nose. There can be muscle twitching and convulsions; in some cases, the dog will develop a thickening of its foot pads. Also, this disease is usually accompanied by pneumonia. If you have reason to believe that your pet has canine distemper, you should see your veterinarian immediately.

Infectious Canine Hepatitis Infectious canine hepatitis is caused by a virus, and it is usually spread by the virus being shed in the urine of affected dogs. Dogs can continue to have contaminated urine even after they have recovered from this disease. This illness is highly contagious, and it can be fatal, even with treatment. The dogs that do recover may have a blue cornea in one or both of their eyes, but this condition will normally clear up within one year. Here are the symptoms to look for:

Affected dogs will run a high fever. They can be listless, and their mucous membranes may be congested. The dog can also lose its appetite, but it may drink enormous amounts of water. If your pet displays these symptoms, do not attempt to treat it at home. See your veterinarian, and the sooner the better.

Leptospirosis This disease is caused by an infectious bacteria, and there are three possible modes of contamination. It is mostly spread through the urine of already affected dogs, but Leptospirosis can also be contracted from contact with infected rat urine. It can even be transmitted by dogs that have recovered. Their urine can remain infectious up to one year after their recovery. You will have to diagnose Leptospirosis quickly, because this is yet another serious disease that can be fatal, even when it is treated.

Look for a loss of appetite, a high fever, depression, and congestion in the whites of the animal's eyes. Affected dogs can also experience jaundice, pain from ordinary movement, vomiting, diarrhea, and a distorted posture when walking. Once you confirm these symptoms, act promptly. See your veterinarian as soon as possible.

Infectious Canine Tracheo-bronchitis Infectious canine tracheobronchitis is also known as para-influenza, and it is commonly called kennel cough. It is a highly contagious condition that affects the upper respiratory system; it is spread through direct or indirect contact with already diseased dogs. While this condition is definitely one of the serious diseases in dogs, it is self-limiting, usually lasting only two to four weeks. There are no permanent side effects if it is caught early, and if the dog is given proper care. So see your veterinarian at the first sign of illness.

The symptoms of infectious canine tracheobronchitis will be obvious. The dog will run a high fever, and it will suffer from intense and harsh coughing fits that bring up mucous. Sometimes the coughing will be so intense that it will prevent the dog from sleeping. As soon as you see that your dog is in trouble, bring it to your veterinarian; and the chances for a complete recovery will be excellent.

Cats   There are four serious diseases that will affect only cats. *Three of them, cat distemper, rhinotracheitis and calici virus, can be prevented by a yearly vaccination. Your cat can be inoculated against all three conditions with just one vaccination.* Do it! Do not let it go. Protect your pet with vaccinations, and you can save its life. The fourth disease, pneumonitis, can also be prevented through inoculation, but it is normally not feasible to do so.

Cat   Cat distemper is also known as feline enteritis or panleucopenia.
Distemper   It is caused by a virus, and affected cats will continually shed this virus in all of their secretions and excretions, making it very contagious. It can be transmitted by direct or indirect contact, and there is a high incidence of fatality in diseased cats. Cats can die, even with treatment. You will have to act quickly, or there will be little chance for your pet to survive.

Cat distemper is characterized by a very high fever, severe depression, vomiting, and diarrhea. It will be obvious that the cat is suffering great distress, and you should see your veterinarian immediately. In young kittens, however, the disease may not be obvious. They can develop peracute conditions (very rapidly) that will kill them overnight, before their condition can be diagnosed. This extremely dangerous disease can even affect unborn kittens.

When expectant mothers have not been vaccinated, cat distemper can develop as an intrauterine infection. This usually results in stillbirth or spontaneous abortion; if the kittens are born alive, they will suffer from kitten ataxia (cerebellar hypoplasia.) The symptoms of this condition are lack of balance, brain damage, and stunted growth. When kittens are born with this disease, they generally die quickly. Those that live should be destroyed. Remember, this deadly disease can be prevented through vaccination, so be sure to protect your cats.

Rhinotracheitis   This disease attacks cats in their upper respiratory tracts, and it can be spread only through direct contact. Some cats will die from this condition, but a large number will recover completely with the proper treatment. You should see your veterinarian as soon as the symptoms become evident.

Affected cats will run a high fever, and they will be obviously sick. There are also a variety of other symptoms that can accompany the fever. Look for sneezing, labored breathing, refusal to eat, dehydration, and a discharge from the animal's eyes and nose. Do not wait too long before you seek professional help. The longer your cat goes without treatment, the less chance it has for survival.

Calici Virus   Calici virus is another dangerous illness that affects cats in their upper respiratory tracts. It is spread mostly by direct contact, but it can also be spread by indirect contact. While this condition will cause some fatalities, most of the cats that are treated early will survive. Fortunately, this disease will generally produce highly visible symptoms.

Calici virus is characterized by high fever, depression, loss of appetite, and dehydration. Affected cats can also sneeze, and exhibit a discharge from their eyes and nose. But the most noticeable symptom will frequently be ulcerations on the cat's tongue. If you believe that your pet has calici virus, you should see your veterinarian immediately, and there will be a good chance for a complete recovery.

Pneumonitis   Pneumonitis is caused by a virus, and like rhinotracheitis and calici virus, this illness also attacks cats in their upper respiratory tracts. It is spread through direct and indirect contact, and it can even develop from a mild cold, when colds are left untreated. Fortunately, pneumonitis is rarely fatal when diagnosed early and given professional attention. Most cats, in fact, will recover completely.

Here are the symptoms that can indicate this disease. Look for sneezing, coughing, loss of appetite, and dehydration. Affected cats may also exhibit a discharge from their eyes and nose. If your pet displays these symptoms, you should see your veterinarian quickly.

This is the one serious disease where immunization will prove to be somewhat impractical. There is an effective vaccine that combats pneumonitis, but it is not widely used because the duration of immunity is too short to provide any kind of reliable, long term protection.

Dogs and Cats Rabies is a deadly disease that affects all warm-blooded animals, including humans. Once an animal (or human) exhibits the symptoms, it is always fatal. *But dogs and cats can usually be prevented from contracting this disease through proper vaccination.* The immunity will last one to three years, depending on the type of vaccine that is used. *See your veterinarian. It is especially important to inoculate your pet against this disease because of the potential danger to you and your family.*

Rabies Rabies is caused by a virus, and this virus is spread through the saliva of an already infected animal, usually through its bite and resulting puncture wound. There are two types of rabies that can affect dogs and cats—dumb and furious. In the furious type, the affected animal can attack anything that moves, including the tires of moving vehicles, people, horses, cattle, etc. In the dumb type, the affected animal will not attack. But both types of rabies will produce the same symptoms.

Rabid dogs and cats will run a high fever, and they will lose their appetites. They will suffer from an inability to swallow that often causes them to drool; they can also develop encephalitis, with convulsions or paralysis. If your pet has rabies, there is no hope. It will have to be destroyed. Protect your pet from this fatal illness with regular vaccinations. See your veterinarian.

Will the proper vaccinations always protect my pet from contracting one of the serious diseases?

It is extremely rare for animals to incur one of the serious diseases after they have been inoculated against it. However, it is possible. If an animal does not receive its first vaccinations at the proper age and regular inoculations thereafter, or if the animal is incubating the disease at the time it is being vaccinated, then it may still contract a particular disease. But even then, it would be highly unlikely to happen.

Do pets ever suffer from an allergic reaction caused by a specific shot or shots? If so, are there substitute vaccines available (for each disease) that will still protect these animals from serious diseases?

The answer to both of these questions is yes. But only a small percentage of pets will ever have an allergic reaction from vaccinations. If your pet is one of them, then your veterinarian will probably try a different brand of vaccine to protect it. In some cases, steroids will be injected at the same time that the animal is being inoculated, and this can be very beneficial in animals that are known to be allergic. Your veterinarian will usually know the procedures to follow if your pet has a history of allergic reactions to various vaccines.

My cat has all of the symptoms of an upper respiratory infection. How long should I continue to treat it at home, before it becomes necessary to see my veterinarian?

This will depend on various factors. If your cat is lively and eating normally, and if the symptoms of its condition are relatively mild, then you can continue home treatment. But if your cat has a fever, or if it is not eating, or if its symptoms are severe, you should see your veterinarian. Do not delay. You should seek professional assistance immediately, or your cat may die. If you have any doubt, you should call your veterinarian, and he or she (or a qualified representative) will guide you.

Do adult cats ever suffer from peracute
respiratory infections?

Not usually. Adult cats can suffer from very acute and severe conditions, but not paracute in the usual sense of the word.

In regard to rabies, where does the term "foaming
at the mouth" come from?

Whenever an animal (or human) is suffering from rabies, it will develop a paralysis in its throat that will prevent it from swallowing. Within a short time, its saliva will become foamy, thus explaining the term.

What should I do if I think my pet has rabies?

Whenever you think that your pet (or any animal) has rabies, you should contact the Public Health Department or a veterinarian. It is extremely important to do this as soon as possible, before the rabid animal can infect another pet or human.

How long does it take for rabies to develop? If I
am bitten by an animal, how long must the
animal be watched, before I can feel safe?

A two-week period of observation is generally considered to be adequate. If you are bitten by an animal, and if it is still normal after two weeks, then you were probably not exposed to rabies. But if you have any doubts regarding whether or not you were bitten by a rabid animal, you should consult your physician.

Skin Diseases and Disorders

For further information, see:
Symptoms   27
Over-the-Counter Medicines   157
NOTE: See "External Parasites" for additional
material on some skin conditions.

Disorders and diseases of the skin can be extremely complex, often reflecting irregularities or dysfunction in other systems and organs of your animal's body. While you can do much to relieve your pet's discomfort, most skin conditions are recurring and some will eventually require some assistance from your veterinarian before they heal.

There are so many causes that complete prevention is almost impossible. The biggest problem is external parasites. Another cause of skin conditions in household pets is improper or inconsistent grooming (see "Basic Pet Care").

Or your pet may suffer from an uncomfortable fungus like ringworm. There are also several kinds of nonspecific fungi that will irritate your animal's skin. Skin problems can result from vitamin deficiences, allergies, and physical contact with chemical irritants such as fuel oils, ice melters, etc.

Even your animal's diet can cause a bothersome skin condition. If your pet eats food it is allergic to, it can develop painful, itchy hives. Sometimes there will be no apparent reason for your pet's unhealthy skin. Your animal may have an organic problem like an improperly functioning thyroid gland that is causing its condition. In rare cases, the reason can even be emotional. There are many skin conditions. Your animal can suffer from a localized condition like raw spots or patches, or a symmetrical disorder (such as dry, dandruffy skin), or even a generalized condition that can affect its entire body.

Fortunately, almost all of these conditions can be easily recognized. If your pet repeatedly scratches, licks, or bites a particular area of its body, look for signs of skin trouble. Is the area dry and raw? Is it inflamed or irritated? If the answer is yes, you should try to determine the cause and begin treatment without delay. In many cases you can relieve your pet's condition entirely. But if the symptom later reappears, the problem may be chronic and you should see your veterinarian.

If you neglect your pet's condition, the animal will continue to bite and scratch the affected area. Soon it will be in danger of self-mutilation. Dogs and cats have ripped out sizeable quantities of hair and skin in an attempt to lessen their discomfort.

If your animal exhibits hairless patches of red, raw, or otherwise disfigured skin, or if its body has moist, oozing hot spots, see your veterinarian immediately. The affected area must be bandaged or protected with collars. Many pets need to be sedated with aspirin or tranquilizers before they will allow the injured area to be examined or touched. It is a troublesome process for both the animal and the owner, and you should never allow your pet's condition to deteriorate this badly.

Once you are aware of your animal's problem, you can start to treat it. Sometimes you can see the cause. For example, if your dog or cat is bothered by fleas, lice, or ticks, they will usually be visible on the animal's body. You can eliminate parasites such as these by using any of the commercial sprays, dips, powders, or shampoos that are available in your pet store. Even if parasites are not directly responsible for your pet's condition, they will certainly aggravate it, and you should remove them as soon as possible.

If your animal has hives, it usually indicates an allergic reaction. Vary your pet's diet or environment (remove plants, etc.) until the condition improves. Once you are certain that the cause has been isolated, correct it. Keep your pet away from anything it seems allergic to. If you cannot determine the cause, your animal's hives may be due to emotional reasons or a dysfunction in one of its internal systems and you should consult your veterinarian.

If your animal's skin is dry and/or inflamed, it could be due to any number of reasons. For example, confined pets on poor diets may develop vitamin deficiencies that can lead to skin trouble. Or your animal could have an internal problem. Contact with chemical irritants and diseases like ringworm are other common causes. You may not always be able to detect and eliminate the cause, but you can begin to ease your animal's discomfort almost immediately.

Try hydrating your animal's skin by soaking it with water. Repeat several times a day. Even better, visit your pharmacy and purchase a container of Domeboro tablets. Follow the instructions on the label to make a soothing medication called Burrow's solution and apply it to your animal's skin as a wet dressing. For local areas of inflammation and irritation, use substances like Solarcaine to temporarily relieve your animal's itching. But if any of these problems persist, you should consult your veterinarian.

Sometimes you can feel a skin condition better than you can see it. Run your hand across your animal's coat. If the skin is dry and/or dandruffy, it needs to be lubricated. One of the best methods of treatment is to mix small amounts of oil into your animal's food.

Many veterinarians have prepared medications that are used expressly for this purpose. Commercial products like Mazola or Wesson oil are also good, and cat owners can even use melted butter. Make sure you use the correct dosage, as outlined in "Over-the-Counter Medicines."

Dry skin is a generalized condition and will usually affect all of your animal's body. One of the symptoms is constant scratching. If your pet suffers from this itchy condition, you will want to relieve it quickly. Mix Alpha-Keri* 1 part to 20 or 1 part to 30 with water and apply with a bottle sprayer like a plant sprayer. Rub the solution into your pet's skin and repeat the process as often as necessary.

To help prevent a dry condition, feed your pet a well-balanced diet. When you buy dog or cat food at the supermarket, check the label. Some products are fortified with vitamins and will help ensure a proper diet. You can also buy a vitamin supplement at your pet store that you can crush or mix into your animal's food.

Dog owners can further prevent dry skin by bathing their pets only when necessary. Contrary to popular belief, frequent baths are harmful to your dog, often causing dry and dandruffy skin. There are ways to wash your dog without endangering its health.

Try wiping them down with damp kitchen towels (not paper towels) at least two or three times a week. This should keep them from becoming dirty or smelly. Also rinsing with water is much less drying than using a shampoo.

If it does become necessary to bathe your dog, stay away from alkaline shampoos (check the label). They will irritate and dry your animal's skin. Instead, use a pH adjusted shampoo obtained from your pharmacy. These shampoos will cleanse your dog without harming its skin.

If your cat or dog continues to have dry skin, or if the condition recedes and reappears, you should see your veterinarian.

Sometimes your pet will suffer from a skin condition and you will be unable to relieve any of the symptoms. Your animal's condition may be due to an infection, fungus, or even an internal problem.

*Alpha-Keri is a nonprescription pharmaceutical product for human beings.

These causes are not detectable by the human eye or touch, and you will have to see your veterinarian for diagnosis and treatment.

My pet seems to shed excessive amounts of hair.
Does this symptom always indicate a skin
problem?

No. In fact, thick-coated dogs like sheperds and collies will normally shed large amounts of hair. Look for hairless patches of skin. Only if you can see bald spots should you consult your veterinarian.

Can a dog or cat suffer bald spots without having
a skin condition?

No, not unless it is a scar. If your pet displays bare patches, it is always indicative of skin trouble. Unlike humans, dogs and cats do not get bald from heredity or age.

Can my pet lose hair from nervousness?

Yes, with an explanation. When animals are frightened (for example, when they are brought to the veterinarian) they will temporarily shed hair at a much faster rate than normal. This is not a dangerous condition, and you should be concerned only when hair loss is accompanied by bald spots.

I have two pets. If one has a skin condition, is the
other one in danger of being affected?

Only those skin diseases that are contagious will be a threat to other animals. Mange, ringworm, and bacterial skin infection are three of the most common examples. If one of your animals seems to have caught a disease from the other (one exhibits symptoms significantly before the other), see your veterinarian. Besides diseases, external parasites like fleas can also be passed as a result of contact with an affected animal.

Are any of an animal's skin conditions
contagious to human beings?

Yes, there are several. Some diseases like sarcoptic mange, ringworm, and various other nonspecific fungi can also be caught by humans. If your veterinarian diagnoses your animal's problem as one of these conditions, you should see your own physician. Additionally, humans can catch poison ivy from an animal that has recently walked, rolled, or laid down in it. And if your pet is bothered by fleas or ticks, your premises may become infested with them. They may then bite you or attach themselves to your leg as you walk through your own home.

Is surgery always necessary whenever an animal displays a cyst or tumor on its body?

To the contrary, surgery is mostly not necessary. Many animals, dogs especially, develop harmless wart-like growths as they become older. There is no danger of malignancy, unless the growth continues to get larger and larger; if that happens, see your veterinarian immediately. In rare cases, a benign growth (as opposed to malignant) will need to be removed because it is impairing one of your animal's functions. For example, if your pet has a large wart on its eyelid, it may have trouble sleeping. Surgery may then be the only cure.

Can I use calamine lotion on my animal's skin to relieve its itching?

Of course. Most soothing lotions and ointments that can be used by humans can also be used by animals. Apply it lightly and rub it completely into your pet's body. Otherwise your pet will lick it off and the itching will continue.

How can I remove ticks from my animal's body?

The easiest way is just to pull them off. This method will leave a small lump on your pet's body, but it is harmless and will heal in about two weeks. You can also use any of the commercial sprays that are available in your pet store, or from your veterinarian. Finally, you can hold a lighted cigarette up to the tick and it will remove itself. But be careful not to burn your animal's fur or skin.

Sprains

For further information, see:

Symptoms	29
Over-the-Counter Medicines	159

Sprains are wrenching injuries that affect one or more of an animal's joints. Simply defined, sprains are a partial rupture (or other injury) of the joint's attachments without displacement of the animal's bones. Although dogs and cats can wrench any of their various joints, they are most often affected in their hip or shoulder joints. They can incur this injury during the course of almost any normal activity.

Pets can hurt their joints from such activities as running, fetching, chasing a ball or stick. They can jump from high places and land improperly or they can turn too quickly while playing or fighting with other animals. There are a multitude of potential causes.

Although sprains are almost impossible to prevent, they are relatively uncommon in household pets. Because dogs and cats use all four limbs for movement, they enjoy better balance than bipeds, and they have less strain on any individual limb. Consequently, they suffer fewer sprains than humans, and the injuries that they do incur are usually not severe. But even minor sprains can be painful and somewhat debilitating, so it is important to recognize and treat your animal's injury as soon as possible. Fortunately, the symptoms will develop quickly, and they are easy to spot.

The area around the injured joint will begin to swell within a very short time after the injury happens. It will continue to swell and may also become inflamed. If you touch the swollen joint, it will feel warm or even hot. In more serious cases, the inflammation will be pronounced and the animal will display great distress. Additionally, the animal will be tentative about putting any weight on the injured limb. It may limp while ambulating, or it may attempt to move while holding the injured limb off the ground, or it may not move at all. Some pets will try to hide from their owners, and others will not. If your pet exhibits the symptoms of a sprain, you should initiate treatment, and the first step is to attend to the animal's swelling.

Swelling and inflammation are best controlled by cold applications, and this method of treatment should be effected as soon as the injury has been diagnosed. Use either cold compresses or an ice pack, and apply gently to the region of the sprain. If your pet does not resist being handled, you can also submerge the injured part in cold water, but make sure you maintain the coldness of the water. Ideally, the sprain should be kept cold for one to two days, but this is not always possible. For best results, change the compresses (or refill the ice pack) whenever they lose their chill. *Do not* use liniments, alcohol, or any of the various commercial rubs on your animal's sprain, because most pets will lick them off soon after they are applied. Not only will this licking and gnawing aggravate the inflammation, but many of these medications are dangerous if taken internally. Once you have controlled the swelling by chilling, the next step is to bandage the sprain.

Wrap the injury with strips of cloth or gauze, and be sure to wrap it fairly snugly. You can also use support or athletic bandages.

Next, tie the ends of the bandage together and fasten the knot with tape. Be sure to secure the bandage in an area that the animal will find difficult to reach. Pets are often annoyed by body wrappings, and they may attempt to bite or scratch themselves free. If your pet does work it loose, you should not wait too long before you rewrap its sprain.

The injured animal will also have to have plenty of rest. Keep your pet in a secluded section of your household and away from any stairs. Try to discourage any unnecessary activity. Within a few days, the injury will usually begin to improve, and the animal will show less distress. In most cases, sprains will heal completely in two to three weeks.

But sometimes the sprain will heal, only to reappear again and again in the same limb. This condition is called a chronic sprain, and it is usually caused by a badly weakened joint that soon begins to succumb to less and less pressure. This condition must be treated differently than normal sprains.

Instead of cold applications, use heat. Apply hot towels or compresses across the affected part. If you have a heat lamp, you can direct it on the wet towels to obtain the maximum benefits. Be sure to change the towels or compresses whenever they lose their heat. But never leave the animal alone when you are using compresses or the heat lamp. You should continue to treat your pet's condition with moist heat until the injury improves. This can take up to several days or even longer, especially when the condition is more severe.

WARNING   If your pet's sprain does not heal, or if the initial symptoms of pain and swelling continue to persevere, or even if these same symptoms are usually severe, you should see your veterinarian. Your dog or cat may be suffering from a fracture* and fractures are serious conditions that require professional attention.

*See "Broken Bones" for further information.

123   Sprains

Do animals ever stretch, rip, or tear their ligaments? If so, how are these conditions treated?

Yes. These injuries can be treated by thoroughly resting the joint (or joints). This can be accomplished by splinting, casting, or bandaging the area, and sometimes by simply confining the injured animal. The specific treatment will depend on the nature and the severity of the injury. If you you think that your pet has injured a ligament, you should consult your veterinarian before attempting to treat it at home.

Do animals ever stretch, rip, or tear their tendons? If so, how are these conditions treated?

Yes. Tendons are the part of the muscle that attaches to the bone, and they can be ripped from their attachments. But animals are more prone to suffer from cut tendons, rather than ripped ones. Tendon injuries heal very slowly, and they should almost always have professional care. If you think that your pet has cut or ripped a tendon, you should consult your veterinarian.

What are the symptoms of ligament and tendon injuries, and how do they differ from those of a sprain?

The symptoms for all of these injuries will be very much alike. For example, they will all cause the affected animal to exhibit pain, swelling, and inflammation. If any of these symptoms are unusually severe, or if they continue to persist after twenty-four hours of home treatment, you should see your veterinarian. He or she will diagnose the specific injury, and then proceed to treat it.

Do animals ever sprain their tails? If so, how is this injury treated?

Yes, an animal's tail joint can be sprained, fractured, or dislocated. Look for the usual symptoms of pain, swelling, and inflammation. The specific injury should be diagnosed by your veterinarian, and it will ultimately need to be bandaged and protected.

Do animals ever suffer from "whiplash," like
humans? If so, how is this injury treated?

This injury will almost never occur in a dog or cat. Whiplash refers specifically to a snapping of the neck vertebrae, and it usually results from a collision with a moving object, like when a car hits something, or is hit itself. This will not normally happen to dogs and cats, because their neck vertebrae are parallel to the ground, as opposed to the vertical vertebrae in humans. Therefore, their necks do not get "snapped" like ours do.

Can animals ever sprain their ribs or pelvis?

It is much more common for an animal to bruise or traumatize its ribs or pelvis, than it is for it to sprain them. However, pets can "sprain" their hip joints or the muscles of their ribcages by overextending or twisting their limbs.

Vitamins and Food Requirements

For further information, see:

Symptoms 30

Over-the-Counter Medicines 161

Even though dogs and cats are classified as carnivorous animals (primarily meateaters,) an all-meat diet will not be sufficient to keep them healthy. Too much meat will not provide the proper bulk, and it usually creates an abundance of phosphorus in the animal's system. This, in turn, can cause the animal to develop uncomfortable and potentially dangerous problems.

In puppies and kittens, for example, excessive phosphorus can lead to poor bone formation and attendant problems such as rickets; and in adult pets, it can lead to weakened bones, generally making them more susceptible to fractures. But these (and other) problems can normally be avoided by feeding your pet well-balanced meals. Fortunately, this is very easy to do.

Many of the commercial pet foods (canned, bulk, or semimoist) are already nutritionally complete. The dog food industry, in particular, has spent large amounts of money to develop these nutritionally complete meals, and they have the test results to prove it. In addition to meat and meat byproducts, pet foods usually contain such things as soybean meal, ground yellow corn, ground whole wheat, and other sources of vegetable protein. Most of these same pet foods are also fortified with extra vitamins and minerals. Look at the label of the pet food that you are currently using. It will probably fulfill your pet's nutritional requirements; if it contains only meat or meat byproducts, you may want to switch brands.

While most of the commercial pet foods are equally sound, some animals may prefer one type of food as opposed to another. For example, one cat may want to eat only a beef and cheese mixture, while another may want to stick to liver and chicken. Dogs and cats do not need variety in their meals in order to thrive, and you should not be wary of offering your pet only one type of food, if it is nutritionally complete, and if it is the only food that your pet will eat. But avoid giving your dog a regular diet of cat food, and vice-versa.

Dogs and cats have different needs, so the nutritional value of dog and cat foods differs accordingly. Cats require more calories per pound of weight (on a daily basis) than dogs do, so their foods are different. Also, cats require an extra amino acid in their foods, while dogs do not. Nutritional needs can even vary from animal to animal within the same species, depending on the age, breed, or lifestyle of the particular dog or cat.

Young, growing animals, hunting and racing dogs, pregnant and nursing mothers, and some older and aging pets may all have specific food requirements. If your animal falls into one of these catagories, you should check its diet with your veterinarian. You may also want to supplement its diet with extra vitamins and minerals. These supplements can be obtained from your veterinarian or your pet store.

Besides commercially prepared pet foods, your animal may also enjoy (or benefit from) other foods that can be added to its regular menu. Human foods such as table scraps can be fed to both dogs and cats, but they should only be given in addition to the animal's regular diet and never as the sole source of nourishment. Try to avoid hand feeding these scraps to your pet, because you may encourage it to beg for food during your meals, or even to jump on the table while you are eating. You should also be careful not to spoil your pet.

Cats (and some dogs) can become very fussy in what they will and will not eat. If you are constantly giving your pet scraps and other treats, it may become "addicted" to these foods, and it may begin to reject the more nutritionally balanced pet foods. Some of the things that commonly cause this problem are liver, fish, chicken, kidneys, and baby food. So be sure to exercise some restraint in regard to table scraps and special treats.

Oils, fats, butter, and margarine can be very good for your animal's coat, but only if they are used in moderation. Raw egg yolks are also good for the coat, and they are an excellent source of protein. Small amounts of these foods can be mixed into commercial pet foods to make them more palatable to your pet, but none of these supplements should be used too freely, or your animal may develop digestive problems or diarrhea.

Other foods that will enhance your pet's diet are raw marrow bones for dogs and raw chicken necks for cats. These bones will help to keep your pet's teeth clean and healthy. You should also supplement your pet's diet with some sort of hard food (like kibble), because these foods are also good for the animal's teeth. Turn to the "Diagnosis and Treatment" section for "Dental Care" for further information.

As long as you continue to feed your pet properly, the animal should remain free from nutritionally based problems. It will be healthy and active, and its coat should be smooth and glossy. If your pet is not on an adequate diet, it will usually exhibit unhealthy symptoms. It may appear to be "pot-bellied" and thin, and its coat can be ragged, dull, and laced with dandruff. Additionally, improper nutrition can eventually cause your pet to suffer from specific conditions like rickets and arthritis. Cats are also susceptible to an uncomfortable condition called steatitis.

Rickets   Rickets is caused by a deficiency of calcium and phosphorus or by calcium and phosphorus in an improper ratio. It occurs mostly in young animals, so if you have a growing puppy or kitten, it is important to feed it well-balanced meals. During the first eighteen months of the animal's life, you should also provide it with vitamin and mineral supplements. If rickets is left untreated, the condition progresses until it becomes irreversible, and the animal will die. Fortunately, the symptoms are easy to recognize, and rickets is relatively easy to correct when it is caught early. Look for bones (or joints) that bend or bow when the animal is walking. If you think that your pet has rickets, see your veterinarian quickly. Prompt diagnosis and treatment are essential if the animal is to survive. Also, you should immediately correct your animal's diet.

Arthritis   Arthritis manifests itself as calcium deposits, usually occuring in the animal's joints. While no one knows all of the causes of this condition, an improperly balanced diet will certainly predispose your pet to it. The symptoms of arthritis are swelling and pain. When the condition occurs in an animal's legs, it may also exhibit difficulty in walking, lying down, and getting up. Unfortunately, arthritis is almost always chronic, and it will continue to reappear. If your pet's condition is severe, you should see your veterinarian; if it is mild, you can attempt to treat it at home by using a substance called Certo.

Certo is a product that is used to make jelly, and it is proclaimed by many owners to be extremely effective in the treatment of arthritis. While there is no medical proof to back this up, there are so many people who recommend its usage that it should certainly be tried. Certo was once sold only as a liquid, but it is now available as a powder. In this form, it can be easily mixed into the animal's food. It has a tart, lemony taste, so you may need to add a small amount of money, syrup, sugar, or another sweetener, before your pet will eat it. See "Over-the-Counter Medicines" for amount and frequency of dosage.

Steatitis

Steatitis is also called yellow fat disease, and it affects only cats. This condition reflects an acute deficiency of Vitamin E. It can occur whenever a cat's diet is limited exclusively to fish (especially tuna), because fish contain enzymes that destroy this vitamin.* The symptoms are easy to spot, and you should see your veterinarian shortly after they appear. The affected cat will run a high fever, and it will display obvious signs of pain and distress. Once your cat has been treated, you should alter its diet. While steatitis can be corrected, it is always better to prevent this condition by feeding your cat a well-balanced diet.

Questions Most Often Asked about Vitamins and Food Requirements

Do dogs and cats ever suffer from an accumulation of cholesterol, like humans?

Yes, but up to now this has not been considered a serious problem. Today's pets, however, are living longer because of better nutrition and general health care. Because cholesterol (when present) usually accompanies the aging process, it may be more of a problem in the near future.

Do animals ever suffer from low blood sugar, like humans?

Yes, but it is fairly rare. The symptoms are dizziness and fainting spells. This condition can only be confirmed through blood tests, so if you think that your animal is affected, you should see your veterinarian. The treatment usually consists of feeding your pet small and frequent meals, comprised of high protein and low carbohydrate (no sugar) foods.

Is it all right to feed my pet ice cream, yogurt, or other milk products?

Yes, but only in small and infrequent portions; and even then, you should stop whenever your pet develops diarrhea from these foods.

*If your cat is allowed outside and is able to catch and eat birds and mice, it will probably be safe from steatitis, even if its regular diet is limited to fish.

Cottage cheese is an excellent milk product, because it provides protein, calcium, and phosphorus.

Is it all right to feed my pet bread, potatoes, or other starchy foods?

Yes, but only in small quantities. Mix these foods into your pet's regular foods. However, it is really unnecessary to supplement your animal's diet with extra starch when well-balanced foods are so readily available.

Do animals ever develop a "sweet tooth," and if so, should it be satiated?

A "sweet tooth" is usually not evident unless the pet has been fed "sweets." You should not satiate your animal's "sweet tooth." More importantly, do not let it develop.

My pet likes to take an occasional drink from my cocktail or my beer glass. Will a small amount of alcohol hurt it?

Small amounts (very small) of alcohol will not usually hurt your pet, but it will not be beneficial either.

What should I do if my pet eats something that disagrees with it and gets a stomach ache?

Dogs and cats will vomit easily, and they may rid themselves of the problem by vomiting the offending material. If not, you can give your animal small amounts of Pepto-Bismol, Kaopectate, or milk of bismuth to help alleviate their problem.

My pet seems to have lost its pep. Can I give it small amounts of Geritol to correct this?

Not really. If a vitamin and mineral supplement is needed, it would be better to use one that is produced specifically for animals and their respective needs. A small amount of Geritol, however, will not be harmful to your dog or cat.

OVER-THE-COUNTER MEDICINES

Prescription for Broken Bones 135

Prescription for Burns 137

Prescription for Common Wounds 140

Prescription for Constipation 143

Prescription for Dental Care 145

Prescription for Diarrhea 146

Prescription for External Parasites 148

Prescription for the Birth Cycle 150

Prescription for Internal Parasites 151

Prescription for Respiratory Infections 153

Prescription for Serious Diseases 156

Prescription for Skin Diseases and Disorders 157

Prescription for Sprains 159

Prescription for Vitamin and Food Requirements 161

This section provides instruction on frequency and dosage for various nonprescription medications. It will help you to treat your pet at home.

Prescription for Broken Bones

For further information, see:

Symptoms 5

Diagnosis and Treatment 35

If your pet is suffering a broken bone, there is very little you can do to ease its pain and discomfort. You can apply ice packs or cold compresses to the injured area to prevent or control swelling. You can confine the animal in a small room to discourage unnecessary movement. You can apply a temporary splint to keep the injured part from moving.

These treatments are explained in the "Diagnosis and Treatment" section for broken bones. But they will only temporarily relieve your pet. If your dog or cat has a fracture, *see your veterinarian.*

For Pain   You can give your dog aspirin, but never give aspirin to your cat.
Dosage:
- For puppies and dogs under ten pounds, 1 baby aspirin or ¼ adult aspirin, three times daily.

- For dogs ten to twenty pounds, two baby aspirins or ½ adult aspirin, three times daily.
- For dogs twenty to thirty pounds, three baby aspirins or ¾ adult aspirin, three times daily.
- For dogs thirty to forty pounds, one adult aspirin, three times daily.
- For dogs forty to fifty pounds, one and ½ adult aspirins, three times daily.
- For dogs fifty pounds and over, two adult aspirins, three times daily.

If you are unable to put the aspirin down your dog's throat, coat it with meat or cheese and the animal will usually eat it. As a last resort, crush it up and mix it with your dog's food.

Note   Aspirin may upset your dog's stomach. If this occurs, discontinue usage.

WARNING   Aspirin is a mild medication that can temporarily relieve your dog's pain. But aspirin is not intended to be a continuing treatment for fracture. If your dog is suffering a broken bone, see your veterinarian for proper diagnosis and treatment as soon as possible.

Prescription for Burns

For further information, see:
Symptoms	7
Diagnosis and Treatment	41

Electrical Burns
Electrical burns should never be treated at home. If your animal is lucky enough to live through this burn, you should take it to your veterinarian without delay.

In some cases, the injured pet will go into shock, and this extremely dangerous condition will have to be attended to even before the burn is treated. Keep your animal warm and see your veterinarian immediately!

Thermal and Friction Burns
While thermal and friction burns have different causes and some dissimilar symptoms, they can each be treated in the same fashion. Either injury can usually be improved by the healing properties in the aloe (or ungentine) plant, or by using Burrow's solution (from Domeboro tablets) as a continous wet dressing. Both of these medications will temporarily relieve the animal's pain and subdue the burn's inflammation.

The aloe plant can be obtained at most plant stores, and it is the thick, jelly-like substance inside the plant that will help your pet. Cut one of the plant's leaves open and remove the substance with your fingertips. Spread it gently over the area of the burn. You should repeat this procedure until the inflammation from the animal's injury is subdued.

Domeboro tablets (or powder) can be purchased at your neighborhood pharmacy. Follow the instructions on the product's label to make a thin, watery solution called Burrow's solution. Use this solution to saturate a small towel (cloth) or a large gauze pad and place the towel against the animal's wound. Next, you will have to secure the towel so that it stays in place.

Take strips of cloth or gauze and wrap them around the saturated towel. Fasten the loose ends in an area that the animal will find hard to reach (and remove). Once the towel is securely in place, it becomes a continous wet dressing.

When the towel dries, remove it and resaturate it in the Burrow's solution or pour the solution directly onto the towel. Then follow the procedure outlined previously to reapply as a wet dressing. Continue to dress your animal's wound until the inflammation goes away.

Do not use Vaseline or any of the various antiseptic medications that are available for humans on your pet's burn. Animals have a tendency to lick off any foreign substances that are put on their bodies, and many of the human lotions or medications are dangerous if taken internally.

Also for Pain   Aspirin will temporarily relieve your dog's pain, but do not give aspirin to your cat. Turn to the "Over-the-Counter Medicines" section for either "Broken Bones" or "Common Wounds" for instruction on correct amounts and frequency of dosage.

WARNING If your animal's thermal or friction burn appears to be unusually severe, or if the symptoms of pain and inflammation do not subside, you should see your veterinarian. Also, if the wound becomes infected, or if the friction burn is accompanied by particles of foreign material that are embedded in the animal's skin, see your veterinarian.

Prescription for Common Wounds

For further information, see:

Symptoms	9
Diagnosis and Treatment	48

Cuts and Lacerations

Make sure that bleeding has been controlled before cleansing the wound or applying medication!

To clean the wound, use any of the following:
- hydrogen peroxide (medical)
- Bactine
- tamed iodine

Apply as needed with a cotton pad or swab, or by washing or soaking.

To disinfect the wound, use any of the following:
- Furacin
- iodine
- Merthiolate

- medicated creams
- Vaseline

Apply with a gauze square or sponge and change the dressing daily, or sooner if dressing becomes wet.

Note Some veterinarians have obtained excellent results by using vitamin E oil (external use only) to treat cuts and lacerations. By applying this oil to the wound, you can help prevent the formation of scar tissue.

WARNING If the wound is gushing blood or if the bleeding cannot be controlled, *consult your veterinarian immediately!*

Abrasions *To soothe irritation,* use any of the following:

- Solarcaine
- Nupercainol
- Unguentine ointment
- Medicated creams
- Calamine lotion
- Vaseline and sulfur

Apply liberally over the affected area with fingertips or by using a gauze or cotton pad.

You can also soothe irritation by applying the surface of aloe plant leaves to the wound *or by* dissolving Domeboro tablets and applying as a wet dressing. *Do not* use internally!

Note Some veterinians have had excellent results by using Vitamin E oil (external use only) to treat abrasions.

Bruises *To reduce or prevent swelling* apply an ice bag or cold compress to the injured area.

For Pain   You can give your dog aspirin, but *never* give aspirin to your cat. The dosage for common wounds is exactly the same as for broken bones and is reprinted here for convenience.

> Dosage:
> - For puppies and dogs under ten pounds, 1 baby aspirin or $1/4$ adult aspirin, three times daily.
> - For dogs ten to twenty pounds, 2 baby aspirins or $1/2$ adult aspirin, three times daily.
> - For dogs twenty to thirty pounds, 3 baby aspirins or $3/4$ adult aspirin, three times daily.
> - For dogs thirty to forty pounds, 1 adult aspirin, three times daily.
> - For dogs forty to fifty pounds, 1 and $1/2$ adult aspirins, three times daily.
> - For dogs that are fifty pounds and over, 2 adult aspirins, three times daily.

If you are unable to put the aspirin down your dog's throat, coat it with meat or cheese and the animal will usually eat it. As a last resort, crush it up and mix it with your dog's food.

Note   Aspirin may upset your dog's stomach. If this occurs, discontinue usage.

WARNING   If your animal's pain is unusually severe and/or if it persists for two or more days, it may suggest a fracture.

Or if your animal holds a limb up, refusing to put weight on it, it may also suggest a fracture.

Consult your veterinarian at once.

Prescription for Constipation

For further information, see:

Symptoms	11
Diagnosis and Treatment	55

There are many ways to cure a constipated pet. For example, you can try a soap (or infant-sized glycerine) suppository or a stool softener like Meta-Mucil. To apply suppositories or glycerine, follow the directions on their containers. The usage of Meta-Mucil is explained in "Diagnosis and Treatment."

But the best treatments have proven to be small amounts of mineral oil or milk of magnesia. These items can be purchased at your local pharmacy or supermarket.

Mineral Oil   Never put mineral oil directly into the mouth of your animal. It is thick and tasteless (like saliva) and may be aspirated into your pet's lungs, causing impaired breathing. Instead, mix it in your pet's food, but be careful to use the right amount.

Dosage

- For small cats, mix ½ teaspoon in its food. For large cats, mix 1 teaspoon. Use this treatment at every feeding until your cat is no longer constipated.
- For small dogs (under fifteen pounds) mix ½ to 1 teaspoon in its food.
- For dogs that weigh fifteen to thirty pounds, mix 1 to 1 and ½ teaspoons.
- For dogs that weigh thirty to sixty pounds, use 1 tablespoon.
- And for dogs that weigh over sixty pounds, use 1 to 2 tablespoons.

Again, keep mixing at every feeding until constipation is no longer present.

Milk of Magnesia

Milk of magnesia can be mixed with your animal's food, or put directly into its mouth—by using an eyedropper or by letting your pet lick it off a spoon.

Dosage:

- For kittens, mix a few drops in milk.
- For cats that weigh five to ten pounds, use ½ teaspoon.
- For cats that weigh ten to twenty pounds, use 1 teaspoon.
- For cats that weigh over twenty pounds, use 1 and ½ teaspoons.
- For dogs that weigh fifteen to thirty pounds, use 1 teaspoon.
- For dogs that weigh thirty to sixty pounds, use 2 teaspoons.
- For dogs that weigh over sixty pounds, use 1 tablespoon.

In all cases (for both dogs and cats) use milk of magnesia no more than one or two times a day. Stop using this medication when constipation has been cured.

WARNING

If, after three or four days of treatment, your animal is still constipated but appears to be eating normally, consult your veterinarian.

Prescription for Dental Care

For further information, see:

Symptoms	12
Diagnosis and Treatment	61

If your animal is suffering from a serious dental problem, you will usually be unable to treat it at home. If you have allowed the condition to deteriorate, or if the problem is being caused by a disease or infection, you will generally need professional assistance to correct it.

In regard to bad teeth and gums, prevention is almost always the optimum care. Turn to "Diagnosis and Treatment" (for "Dental Care") where your preventative program has already been outlined.

For Pain in Dogs You can give your dog aspirin to temporarily relieve its pain and discomfort, but never give aspirin to your cat. Turn to the "Over-the-Counter Medicines" section for either "Broken Bones" or "Common Wounds" for correct amounts and frequency of dosage.

Prescription for Diarrhea

For further information, see:

Symptoms   14

Diagnosis and Treatment   68

When your animal is suffering from diarrhea, treat it with small amounts of Pepto Bismol or Kaopectate.

Both of these medications can be purchased at your supermarket or your drugstore.

Dosage

- For kittens, give ¼ teaspoon every four hours.
- For cats, give ½ teaspoon every four hours.
- For dogs twenty pounds or under, give 1 teaspoon every four hours.
- For dogs over twenty pounds, give 1 tablespoon every four hours.

The medicine can be given to dogs by mixing it in their food, or by letting them lick it directly from the spoon.

Cats, however, may refuse to eat "doctored food," and they will probably react badly to the threat of a spoon. You can administer the medicine by using an eyedropper and inserting it gently into your cat's mouth.

WARNING   If your animal's diarrhea continues to persist after twenty-four hours of treatment, or if there is evidence of blood in the diarrhea, consult your veterinarian.

Prescription for External Parasites

For further information, see:

Symptoms 15

Diagnosis and Treatment 73

Fleas, ticks, and lice can be controlled and often eliminated by any of the various parasite sprays, dips, baths, and powders that are available in your pet store. Fleas can also be controlled through the use of flea collars and medallions.

Make sure that the product you choose to use applies to the specific parasite that is affecting your animal. Also, make sure the product's label specifies use for cats before you use it on your cat.

When treating fleas, ticks, and lice be sure to also decontaminate your premises. Otherwise, your pet may become reinfested.

Any of these parasites can cause your animal to suffer related skin conditions. See "Skin Diseases and Disorders" for further information.

Maggots and mites (sarcoptic, demodectic and ear mites) will require professional attention before they can be eliminated.

Mites are invisible to the human eye and will always cause your pet to suffer related skin conditions. If your pet is infested by mites, it will display bothersome symptoms like scratching or biting the affected area. You can temporarily relieve these symptoms, but the animal's condition will soon reappear.

If this is the case, see your veterinarian. Your animal may be suffering from mites or even a more serious problem. The only way to know for sure is through a professional examination.

Prescription for the Birth Cycle

For further information, see:

Symptoms   17

Diagnosis and Treatment   79

There are no commercial medications that should be given to your female pet to aid her during heat or pregnancy. But it is important to remain in contact with your veterinarian during the entire birth cycle. If your pet develops complications, or if she contracts a nonrelated condition that requires professional attention, your veterinarian will prescribe the proper treatment.

Prescription for Internal Parasites

For further information, see:

Symptoms   19

Diagnosis and Treatment   90

There are several commercial vermicides and preventative worm medicines that are available through your pet store or veterinarian. You may want to try a "once-a-month wormer." There is even an effective mixture that will prevent roundworms, hookworms, and heartworms in the same dosage. But before you apply any of these remedies to your dog or cat, you should speak with your veterinarian.

Each internal parasite must be eliminated with a medicine that was specifically designed to kill it. Otherwise, the problem may persist. You should also be careful not to use any of these medicines in excessive amounts, or it may be fatal. So rely on your veterinarian. In virtually all cases of infestation, the diagnosis and treatment should be done by a professional.

A Common Myth Some people believe that feeding garlic to an infested animal will kill its worms. This is simply not true. If it were that easy to eliminate parasitic worms, veterinarians would never see them in dogs and cats. Do not depend on folklore to cure an infested pet. See your veterinarian.

Prescription for Respiratory Infections

For further information, see:
Symptoms   22
Diagnosis and Treatment   101

Many of the respiratory infections that affect dogs and cats are nonserious conditions that can produce mild symptoms like sneezing and coughing. Some of these symptoms can be treated and relieved at home, and the infection itself will usually improve within several days.

If the condition persists, however, or if the symptoms are unusually severe, you should see your veterinarian.

To Relieve Congestion   You can often loosen your pet's congestion by using a vaporizer. It is usually best to confine the animal in a small room while the vaporizer is at work. If your vaporizer has a compartment for medications, use Vick's VapoRub or a similar remedy. Generally, the strength of the medication and the frequency of usage should be the same as for a human baby.

Also, if your dog is congested, you can give it Contac or a similar cold medication for humans. Coat the medication with meat or cheese and your dog will probably gobble it down.

Dosage:
- For dogs five to fifteen pounds, use ¼ of the human dosage.
- For dogs fifteen to thirty-five pounds, use ½ of the human dosage.
- For dogs thirty-five pounds and over, use the full human dosage.

If the medication is in the form of time release (like Contac), repeat once a day until the condition improves. Otherwise, follow the frequency instructions on the product's label. If the animal's condition does not improve within several days, see your veterinarian.

To Relieve Sinus Conditions

Dogs and cats will sometimes suffer chronic sinus conditions with uncomfortable symptoms like snorting and difficulty in breathing. You will not be able to relieve your cat, but you may be able to relieve your dog.

One of the best treatments is a product called Sinutab. This is a nonprescription medication for humans that can be obtained at your pharmacy.

You should coat the medication with meat or cheese so your dog will swallow it.

Dosage:
- For dogs five to fifteen pounds, use ¼ tablet.
- For dogs fifteen to thirty-five pounds, use ½ tablet.
- For dogs thirty-five pounds and over, use 1 tablet.

Repeat the correct dosage two or three times a day until your pet's condition improves. If the infection persists after several days of treatment, you should see your veterinarian.

To Relieve Coughing

You can relieve your dog's cough with any of the over-the-counter cough medicines for humans that can be obtained at your supermarket or pharmacy. These medications should not be used on cats.

Let your dog lick the medication off a spoon. If the animal resists, put the medicine directly into its mouth by using a spoon or an eyedropper. This can be done by tilting the dog's jaw upward and applying pressure until the animal's mouth is open. Once open, insert the medication and the dog will usually swallow it.

Dosage:
- For dogs five to fifteen pounds, use ¼ of the human dosage.
- For dogs fifteen to thirty-five pounds, use ½ of the human dosage.
- For dogs thirty-five pounds and over, use the full human dosage.

Follow the frequency instructions on the product's label and continue usage until the condition improves. If coughing persists after several days of treatment, you should see your veterinarian.

For Pain   You can give your dog aspirin to temporarily relieve its pain and suffering, but never give aspirin to your cat. Turn to "Over-the-Counter Medicines" for either "Broken Bones" or "Common Wounds" for correct amounts and frequency of dosage.

WARNING   Some symptoms are extremely serious, and you should not attempt to treat them at home. If your dog or cat is obviously sick (displays symptoms like lethargy and loss of appetite) with a fever of 103 degrees or over, you should see your veterinarian as soon as possible. Do not wait two or three days to see if the condition improves. Your animal may need prompt attention.*

*See "Serious Diseases" for further information.

Prescription for Serious Diseases

For further information, see:

Symptoms   24

Diagnosis and Treatment   107

None of the serious diseases should be treated at home. As soon as your pet exhibits any of the symptoms, you should see your veterinarian. Do not delay. Many of these diseases can be fatal, even with treatment.

Of course, the best treatment is prevention. So be sure to protect your pet with regular vaccinations.

Prescription for Skin Diseases and Disorders

For further information, see:

Symptoms	27
Diagnosis and Treatment	115

The treatment of skin diseases and disorders can be an unsatisfying process. You can often relieve the symptoms without actually correcting the problem. In some cases, the symptoms will also persist.

If your animal's condition fails to improve after several days of treatment, or if it appears to recede and then recurs at a later date, you will have to consult your veterinarian.

To Relieve Itching Spray Solarcaine (or a similar medication) on the affected area and repeat as often as necessary.
There are also several good commercial products that will soothe your animal's itchy skin. They are available at your pet store or pharmacy.

To Relieve Dry, Dandruffy Skin

Dry skin needs to be lubricated. You can help your animal correct this condition by mixing small amounts of Mazola or Wesson oil into its food. Cats especially love melted butter.

Mix the oil into your animal's meal and repeat once a day until the condition improves.

Dosage:
- For small dogs and cats (under fifteen pounds) mix ½ teaspoon.
- For dogs and cats that weigh between fifteen and thirty-five pounds, mix 1 teaspoon.
- For animals that weigh more than thirty-five pounds, mix 1 tablespoon.

WARNING

If any of these oils or butter cause your pet to suffer from diarrhea, you should reduce the amounts.

Prescription for Sprains

For further information, see:

Symptoms   29

Diagnosis and Treatment   121

Sprains are treated in much the same way as broken bones, and like fractures, there is little you can do to aid your animal's convalescence.

You can chill the injured region with cold compresses or ice packs to subdue and control swelling.

You can bandage the sprain to give it rest and support during the healing period.

You can monitor your pet's activities to ensure that it gets plenty of rest.

But never use alcohol, liniment, or any of the commercial rubs on your pet's sprain, because they can be dangerous if ingested into the animal's system.

All of these treatments are thoroughly explained in "Diagnosis and Treatment," and you should read this section carefully before attempting to treat your animal's sprain.

For Pain   You can give your dog aspirin, but never give aspirin to your cat. Turn to the "Over-the-Counter Medicines" section for either "Broken Bones" or "Common Wounds" for correct amounts and frequency of dosage.

WARNING   Sprains and fractures can cause similar symptoms, but fractures are a more serious condition, and they usually need professional assistance to mend. If your pet is still in great pain after twenty-four hours of treatment, or if the injury does not improve, or if the inflammation and swelling do not subside, consult your veterinarian. You may have mistakenly diagnosed the injury as a sprain, when your animal may really be suffering from a broken bone.*

*See "Broken Bones" for further information.

Prescription for Vitamins and Food Requirements

For further information, see:

Symptoms	30
Diagnosis and Treatment	126

In most cases, the conditions (and symptoms) that result from poor nutrition are eased and even corrected by altering the animal's diet. If you feed your pet well-balanced meals, you can usually prevent any of these conditions from developing. As always, prevention is the most effective cure.

For Arthritis While there is no medical substantiation, many people believe that you can relieve arthritic pain by giving affected animals a product called Certo. Purchase some Certo in powdered form, and mix it into the animal's food. You should continue to use this product until the pain has been relieved.

Dosage:

- For small dogs and cats, use 1 teaspoon, two times daily.
- For medium-sized dogs, use 1 tablespoon, two times daily.
- For large dogs, use 2 tablespoons, two times daily.

Also for Arthritic Pain   You can give your dog aspirin, but never give aspirin to your cat. Turn to the "Over-the-Counter Medicine" section for either "Common Wounds" or "Broken Bones," for instruction on administering it.

WARNING   If your pet's arthritis is severe, do not attempt to treat it at home. See your veterinarian.

HOUSEHOLD PETS

Your Veterinarian 165
How to Use Your Pet Store 168
Basic Pet Care 173

This section contains special chapters on household pets, including information on your veterinarian, your pet store, and basic pet care.

Your Veterinarian

Whenever your pet is in need of professional attention, your veterinarian will be the person who supplies it. It is extremely important to develop a good relationship, because you and your veterinarian will have to work together in order to help your pet. But first, you will have to find a qualified doctor who is within easy access.

If you already own an animal and are about to move, you should ask your current veterinarian to recommend a good doctor who is located in your new area. But if you are about to become a new pet-owner, or if you want to change veterinarians (for any reason), you will have to use other sources.

You can look through the yellow pages, or you can check with your local (or county) veterinary association. In addition, many pet stores now keep lists of qualified doctors and they are grouped according to neighborhood. If you frequent one of these pet stores, you can ask them for a recommendation or you can ask your physician or dentist. You can even ask animal-owning friends for the name of their veterinarian, but unless you respect their opinion, you should find your doctor through a different source.

Once you have acquired the name of a good veterinarian, you should call his or her office for some preliminary information, and you should do this before you make your first visit. Be sure that the doctor's hours will coincide with your schedule, and you may want to determine the cost of an examination or an office visit. It is also important to discuss the terms of payment.

A few veterinarians will issue credit from the very first visit, many others will not, and some will never give credit. Some will take credit cards, but a majority will not. Most veterinarians, however, will accept personal checks, but not always on the first visit. So be prepared to pay cash unless you have inquired in advance. Remember, neither you nor your veterinarian will benefit from a misunderstanding, so check out the office policy before you go.

After you are satisfied, you can set up your first visit. It is usually better to make an appointment rather than to just show up with your pet. Otherwise, you may have to waste valuable time by sitting in the waiting room. Try to be prompt. If you are going to be late, try to notify your doctor's office. If they are aware of the problem, they may still be able to accommodate you without making you wait. Even in cases of emergency, you should still call ahead. If your veterinarian cannot see you quickly, he or she will recommend an alternate doctor or a nearby clinic.

Once you and your animal are in the veterinarian's office, you should tell him or her exactly what you think the problem is. Be direct and honest. Do not be embarrassed if your pet's condition is due to owner neglect or a lack of knowledge. Your veterinarian is there to help you, and your main concern should be the health of your animal. If you have any questions while your animal is being examined, ask them. If you do not understand any of the answers, ask your veterinarian to be more explicit. Most veterinarians are extremely conscientious, and they will be glad to give you the needed information.

In some cases, you will be unsure as to whether or not your pet needs professional attention. Call your veterinarian and describe its condition. You may be able to treat the problem at home, or it may be necessary to schedule a visit. If you have general questions regarding your animal's health, you should contact your veterinarian's office for the answers. In many cases, the information can be supplied by receptionists, technicians, or other trained personnel. When it is necessary to speak to the veterinarian, you will either be connected or your call will be returned.

How to Use Your Pet Store

While everyone knows that animals and pet supplies can be purchased at pet stores, very few people are aware of the variety of services and goods that many of these pet shops have to offer. They can, for example, special order unusual animals like baby skunks. They can supply you with a breath freshener for your dog. They can sell you a blood coagulant, in case you cut into the quick (blood supply) while you are clipping your animal's toenails. You can even secure a repellent that will discourage your cat from damaging your furniture. All you have to do is ask.

Of course, the availability of various services, animals, and related products may depend on the season or the type of pet store you choose to supply you. For example, certain kinds of birds can only be obtained one or two months out of the year, and even then, the supply may not meet the demand. Additionally, there are three distinctly different kinds of pet stores, and they all offer varying degrees of service. There are full-service, limited-service, and speciality shops, and animal-owners should be aware of how each one functions in order to best ensure that their specific needs are fulfilled.

The
Full-Service
Pet Store

Full-service pet shops usually offer the widest scope of animals and related products. They tend to have better access to all kinds of pets, as well as hard goods.* Because the employees of full-service shops have to sell and care for many different animals, they tend to be well trained and highly knowledgeable. Many of these employees will be able to give you sound advice. They can suggest the type of pet that would be right for you and your life style, and they can often provide good instruction on health care and grooming. In fact, most of the full-service stores will offer their own grooming service.

Limited-
Service
Pet Stores

Limited-service pet stores tend to have less knowledgeable employees, fewer services, and a smaller selection of pets and related supplies than full-service shops. While this type of store will usually carry dog-and cat-related products (collars, leashes, dishes, etc.), they will rarely offer dogs and cats for sale. Instead, most of these stores concentrate on smaller pets like hamsters and birds. Occasionally, a limited-service shop will obtain an unusual bird or a hard-to-find rodent (such as black gerbils), but more often than not, you will have to visit your full-service shop to obtain these pets. Limited-service shops are usually found in department stores or small shopping malls, and they almost never offer a grooming service.

Speciality
Pet Stores

Specialty pet stores concentrate on one type of animal, like cats or reptiles. Some of these stores will focus all of their energy on one breed within a species, such as Persian cats. If you have highly specialized needs, then this is the type of shop to use. Any establishment that deals exclusively with one type of pet will generally

*Hard goods is the term that is generally applied to pet supplies and other related products.

have the best available selection of those pets and their related products. But they will sell only the hard goods that are produced for their particular kind of animal. Specialty shops that cater to cats often provide grooming and boarding, and their employees are usually qualified to give sound advice on diet and general health care.

Regardless of the type of pet store that you decide to patronize, you will want to get the maximum benefit out of what is available. There are several kinds of services that you can utilize, if you know what to ask for. Here is a descriptive list of those services that will enable you to get the full use out of your pet shop:*

Purchasing a Pet
It is usually best to purchase your animal directly from a professional breeder or a reputable pet store. If your pet store guarantees their animals to be in good health (without hidden physical defects), then you can purchase one of their animals without worry; but be sure that you can return or exchange the pet if it is not in good health. Many pet stores buy their animals from highly competent breeders, so this will not usually be a problem. Even when pet stores take their animals from amateur or noncommercial breeders, they usually do so only if the pets have been examined and have had their first vaccinations. Once you decide to buy a certain animal, pet shop personnel can tell you all about it. They can tell you what breed your dog or cat is and how large it will be when it reaches maturity. This is something you cannot be sure of if you answer a "puppies (or kittens) for sale" ad in the newspaper. If you are buying a smaller animal, like a rodent or a bird, you can be assured that the health control imposed on your pet shop is as stringent as the control that governs their sale of dogs and cats.

Choosing a Pet
In some cases, prospective owners will be unsure of what kind of animal to buy. They may need a pet that can spend much of its time alone. Or they may want an animal that needs very little space. Conversely, they may want a pet that requires a lot of attention and space. There are other questions, too. Which animals shed?

*All of the services that are listed are normally available through full-service shops, and particular limited-service and specialty shops may offer one or more of them, unless otherwise specified.

What kinds of pets will tend to be nervous or high strung? If you want to know which animal will best suit your needs, ask your pet shop people. They should be able to answer all of your questions. With the help and guidance of your pet shop personnel, you can usually acquire an animal that is just right for you.

General Health Advice

Pet store owners and their employees can give very good advice in regard to basic health and care. This is especially true in full-service shops. They can tell you when to see your veterinarian, and they can suggest certain nonprescription drugs and dietary aids for less serious conditions. If you need a vitamin supplement, an oil for your animal's coat, or any of the other hard goods that will help to keep your pet healthy, they can recommend a good product. But most importantly, they can tell you how to care for your animal on a daily basis. This kind of regular care can be quite effective in combating illness. Pet shop personnel can also be very knowledgeable in regard to birds and other small animals. But whenever there is a possibility that your pet is suffering from a serious condition, you should consult your veterinarian.

Referral Service

Almost every full-service pet shop will have a list of reputable veterinarians. If you need a veterinarian to attend to your animal, they will refer you to one that lives in your neighborhood. This referral service is especially important to new pet owners who will need to have their animals vaccinated when they reach the right age. Some specialty shops may also offer this service, but it is almost never offered by limited-service stores. In addition to veterinarians, many pet shops will have referral lists for boarding kennels and qualified groomers. Full-service shops, however, will usually perform these services themselves, inside their premises.

Grooming

Full-service pet stores are usually the only kind of pet shop that will offer a grooming service. Some dogs, like poodles, will need to have their coats trimmed frequently. This will not only help them to keep neat and clean, but it will also help them to avoid skin diseases. Unless you have had some experience in trimming animals, you should leave the grooming of your dog to your pet store.

The only cats that may ever need to have their hair cut are the long-haired varieties. These cats need frequent brushing or their hair can mat. When this happens, it must be cut. A trained groomer will remove the matted hair but will not cut hair from any other area of the animal's coat. Since mats usually occur in hard-to-get-at places (the stomach, behind the ears, underneath the chin, etc.), this job should be done by an expert. Leave it to your pet store.

Besides trimming and cutting, full-service pet stores usually offer the whole gamut of other grooming services. They can clip your pet's nails, clean its teeth, give your dog a bath, etc. You can trust any of these jobs to your well-trained pet shop groomer.

Special Orders

Full-service pet stores will have access to an enormous variety of hard goods, and they may be able to procure certain birds and animals from all over the world. If you need a particular product and do not see it in your pet shop, ask for it. If it exists, it can be specially ordered for you. Birds and other animals, however, can be somewhat harder to obtain by special order. The availability of these pets can fluctuate greatly, depending on the season, supply, demand, and import laws.* Your full-service shop can also special order certain wild animals, like foxes, skunks, ferrets, raccoons, and others.† But many pet shops will refuse to do this, on the basis that wild animals do not usually make good pets when they are confined in captivity. Additionally, some states now require owners to secure permits to harbor and confine wild animals, even if they obtained them as orphaned young.

*For example, several years ago it was easy to obtain a cockatoo. But now, because of the import laws, it is extremely difficult. If you do succeed in getting one, the cost is likely to be very high.

†Many states have laws that govern the sale of wild animals as pets. For example, in New York state it is illegal for pet stores to sell foxes.

Basic Pet Care

There are several elements of basic pet care that can help to prevent dogs and cats from contracting diseases and other uncomfortable conditions. While the pet-owner is not expected to have professional expertise regarding care and grooming, he or she can still follow certain procedures that will help to keep their animals healthy.

This chapter will provide good instruction on grooming and bathing your pet, and on trimming its nails and hair. It will also provide some general information on other kinds of basic pet care.

Grooming As your animal's coat undergoes the constant process of renewal, the old hair is shed and is caught in the new hair. If the dead hair is allowed to accumulate, it can become matted in the animal's fur, often causing the skin underneath the matted area to stretch tighter and tighter. Eventually, this may cause the animal to develop sores and lesions, with resultant itching and discomfort. This in turn, can lead to a number of unhealthy conditions.

Affected pets will usually have a bad appearance, and they may also exhibit an unpleasant odor. But more importantly, they can develop various skin conditions, and even some related internal problems that can hamper their digestion and elimination. In some cases, a lack of grooming can also make your pet more susceptible to external and internal parasites.

For example, as your animal tries to relieve the constant irritation (from the sores or lesions), it can bite, scratch, or tear at its skin. This usually results in bare spots or other skin conditions. Additionally, the animal may lick the affected area, and as it does so, it may inadvertently swallow large amounts of dead hair. Once ingested, this hair can form into hairballs and cause the animal to have digestive or elimination trouble. Finally, external parasites will find ideal nesting conditions in tangled and dirty fur; the eggs of internal parasites are easily caught in dirty coats, and carried until the animal licks them off and swallows them.*

Of course, a lack of good grooming will not always cause these conditions, but it is extremely important to protect your pet by keeping it clean. The first step is to secure the proper tools.

The basic equipment is a brush and a comb, and they must be well suited to your pet's coat. For short-haired animals, use a short-bristled brush, but for long-haired pets, like Persian cats or collies, use a slicker brush. The comb should be fine, medium, or coarse, depending on the thickness of your animal's coat. Long-haired pets may need two combs, a coarse comb for an initial combing and a fine-toothed comb to apply the finishing touches. You will be able to find a wide assortment of these combs and brushes at your pet store.

*If your pet suffers from any of these conditions, they will have to be treated independently of good grooming. See "Skin Diseases and Disorders," "Constipation," "External Parasites," or "Internal Parasites" for further information.

Of course, even if you have the proper tools, your pet will have to be at ease with the prospect of being groomed. It is best to start brushing and combing an animal's coat while it is still a puppy or kitten. A daily grooming session (regardless of whether the animal needs it or not) will quickly accustom young pets to this sort of handling. If you do not begin to groom your animal until it grows older, it may be less likely to tolerate this procedure. Even so, there are ways to alleviate its nervousness. Handle it gently and pet it lightly. Continue to pet it and talk to it softly until it appears to be calm. Then put it on a table so you will have good balance and maximum control of its movements. Now you are ready to begin the grooming.

You can enhance the soothing atmosphere by beginning to brush it with short, quick strokes. But do not brush along the lay of the fur because the brush will merely slip over the coat's surface without really penetrating. Use your short strokes to brush up the fur against the grain; this will remove much of the dirt and dead hair that has caught below the top layer of the animal's coat. Do not use excessive force and be especially gentle with tender areas, such as the stomach and behind the ears. When most of the loose material has been removed, smooth the hair back into place by going with the lay. Once the fur has been properly smoothed, you can begin to comb it.

The teeth of the comb will separate the animal's fur and remove any dirt or dead hair that the brush may have missed. Comb against the grain at first, using short strokes, as in brushing. When you are through combing, go with the lay to smooth the fur. Once again, you should not use too much force, and remember to be very gentle whenever you are grooming through the tender areas.

For best results, you should continue to brush and comb your pet on a daily basis, engaging in a longer and more thorough session about once or twice a week. After brushing smooth-coated dogs (dobermans, boxers, etc.) and short-haired cats, you can wipe them down with a damp, terrycloth towel. This will help to keep their coats clean by removing street dust and excess oils.

As you are grooming your pet, you may occasionally see sores, cuts, or rashes on its skin. You will have to treat these problems as separate conditions.* You may also encounter tangled or matted hair, and you will have to know how to remove it.

The tangle will probably catch in the teeth of your comb, but you should resist any urge to yank the comb through it. A hard yank can uproot the hair, often leaving bare spots. It can also cause your pet to suffer unnecessary pain. Fortunately, there is a better way to eliminate these clumps of hair. Hold the comb tightly behind the tangle, and clip it off with a pair of scissors. Be sure to cut against the comb (between the mat and the comb), and this will prevent you from accidentally cutting into your animal's skin. The procedure is exactly the same for removing mats.

When to Bathe Your Pet

Good grooming entails more than brushing and combing. You may also need to give your pet a bath. First, you must determine whether or not your animal needs it. Dogs will usually require bathing more often than cats, and there are some good indications to guide you.

If your dog is obviously dirty or if it has a bad odor, it will usually benefit from a bath. But there are other factors, too. Its lifestyle and breed can also dictate the necessity of being bathed.

Indoor dogs, for example, will normally need fewer baths than outdoor dogs. But if your indoor pet spends a lot of time in a dusty basement (or other dirty areas), then you will have to bathe it more often. Additionally, smooth-haired dogs may need bathing only once or twice a year, while long-haired pets may need it every few months, or even more. You will have to exercise good judgment and discretion, because too-frequent bathing can strip your dog of its protective oils and dry its skin. If you are unsure, you should consult your veterinarian.

Cats, however, should be bathed only under the most extreme

*Turn to "Skin Diseases and Disorders" and "Common Wounds" for further information.

circumstances (like being sprayed by a skunk), because they are normally fastidious and will do the job themselves. Cats have rough tongues that are covered with spicules, or little bumps. As the cat licks itself, these spicules will help to separate the hairs in their fur and remove dirt and dead hair, just like a comb. So be sure your cat needs a bath before you give it one.

The Bath Once you have decided to bathe your pet, you may find that the animal will be resistant to your efforts. Some animals like to be put in water, and others do not. If your pet struggles, you should try to relieve its anxiety by making the bath as pleasant as possible. While there is no sure method of doing this, the owner will usually be able to calm his or her animal by following some simple guidelines.

Fill a receptacle with several inches of lukewarm water. If the water is too hot or too cold, it may alarm the animal and cause it to suffer some discomfort. Also, you should make sure that the water is not too deep. Your pet will probably be more secure if the water level is no higher than its stomach. Next, lower your animal slowly into the water and be careful to support its front and hind quarters as you do so. If you own a large breed of dog, it may be easier to reverse the order. Start by placing your pet into an empty receptacle, and then add the water. But be sure to add the water gradually, as too much noise and splashing may frighten your dog and cause it to struggle.

Of course, the best way to soothe your animal is to reassure it with petting and soft words. You should continue to do this until the animal is calm. Once your dog or cat has become acclimated, you can begin to bathe it.

Cup some of the water into your hands and pour it slowly over the animal's back. You can also use a sponge or cloth to wet its hair. After the coat is wet, you can apply a shampoo and work it into a lather. Be sure to use a mild, pH-adjusted liquid shampoo, because alkaline shampoos may cause your pet to develop a dry and dandruffy skin condition.

Next, use your hands to work the lather through the animal's coat and around its body, but avoid the area around your pet's eyes. If you do get soap in its eyes, rinse them with clean water, until the animal is out of distress. After the coat has been well lathered, you should rinse it thoroughly with clean water. Do not leave any traces of shampoo on the animal's body, because dry shampoo can dull its coat; it may also make the animal itch, with resulting skin problems. Before you remove your pet from the tub, you can rinse any remaining shampoo from its body and legs. Make sure that all of the soap is gone. You can use a water spray, but be careful, because this device may frighten your animal, making it more reluctant to take future baths. After your pet has been completely rinsed, it will have to be dried. This is the final step in the bathing process.

Wrap a terrycloth towel around your animal's body, and rub it briskly through its fur. Keep rubbing until the animal is fairly dry and remove the towel. Your pet may want to complete the job by shaking off any excess water, and you should allow it to do this. Some owners use hand-held hairdryers to speed up the drying, but if your pet is frightened by the noise, or the hot, blowing air, you should not use it. Even if your animal accepts the dryer, you should still be cautious. Make sure that the setting of the instrument is at a low heat. Dry the animal in a warm room that is free from drafts.

WARNING If your dog still has a bad odor after being bathed, you should consult your veterinarian. This can be indicative of a skin condition, and if so, you will want to have it treated.

After the Bath When you have finished bathing your pet, you may want to clean its eyes and ears, and this is a good time to do it. Of course, you should clean your animal's ears about once a month, whether or not you have just given it a bath.

Moisten a cotton swab with mineral oil and insert it gently into your pet's ear. Without making exaggerated movements, turn it a little to collect the excess wax. If your animal's ears are very dirty, you may have to use more than one swab.

In addition to wax, poodles and terriers may have excess hair growing in their ear canals. Fortunately, this hair is soft and fuzzy, and it is usually easy to remove it. Hold the hair firmly between your thumb and forefinger, and with a twisting motion, pluck it out. But be sure to pluck out only the hair that is growing in the ear canal. If you yank at the hair on the edge of the canal or on your pet's ear, you may cause your pet to suffer some pain.

It is also good to make an occasional inspection of your animal's eyes. If you can see any discharge, you should wipe it away with a damp, terrycloth towel, and be sure to keep your pet's eyes dry.

Nail Trimming

Cats will normally shed their nails, so they will almost never need to have them clipped (unless you want to protect your furniture, or other possessions). Dogs, however, should have their nails clipped whenever they are "clicking" on the floor as the dog is walking. Like brushing and combing, this procedure should be initiated while the animal is still young and continued on a regular basis throughout its life. But before you do it, be sure to have the proper equipment.

Do not use razor blades or a pair of scissors on your pet's nails because they can be awkward to handle, and you may accidentally injure your animal. Use a nail clipper instead.

Your pet store should offer several different sizes of clippers, so you will be able to obtain the right tool for your particular dog or cat. Hold the animal's limb firmly with one hand and clip its nails with the other. But be very careful. The blood supply runs through each of your pets claws, and if you cut into it, the animal will bleed. If you are unsure or inexperienced, ask your veterinarian to show you the best way to hold your pet and exactly where to cut to avoid the vein. You can also purchase a coagulant at your pet store; it is a good idea to have one on hand before you begin to clip the nails. If an accident does happen, the coagulant will stop the flow of blood.

Trimming Your Dog's Hair

One of the most difficult aspects of basic pet care is trimming your animal's hair. Although this procedure can be learned and can be performed at home, it is almost always better to leave it to a professional groomer. The need for trimming your dog's hair will depend greatly on what breed it is. Some breeds, like dachshunds and other smooth-haired dogs, never need to be trimmed. Other dogs, like poodles and schnauzers, require frequent trimmings. If you decide to attempt this job at home, you can ask your veterinarian for the correct procedures to follow, but it may be better to pay a professional groomer to teach you how to do it.

Trimming Your Cat's Hair

Cats, even the long-haired breeds, never need to have their hair cut. In some cases, their fur can mat or tangle, but the procedure for removing these clumps of hair, has already been outlined in this chapter under "Grooming."

Altering or Castration

Some pet-owners are reluctant to alter their males because they fear that altering will have an adverse effect on their pets. This is simply not true. In fact, altering your animal will prove to be mostly beneficial, and there are many reasons to do it.

For example, when male pets are neutered, they will usually live longer, and many veterinarians believe that they will also make better pets. They will tend to have fewer fights with other male animals and will therefore suffer fewer wounds and abcesses. Moreover, if the dog or cat is an outdoor pet, altering will prevent it from roaming for sexual reasons, and it will stay closer to home. Besides all of the above, cats should be altered for another reason.

The urine of male cats has a strong pungent odor, and the animal will spray its urine (even indoors) to mark its territorial boundaries. But a neutered cat will not normally spray, and the urine will lose its odor.

Both dogs and cats should be altered when they are about ten or eleven months old, but while it is better to neuter dogs when they are still young, the surgery can be performed safely at any age, as long as they are mature with normal body development.

Vasectomies   Vasectomies, like altering, will succeed in making your animal sterile, but they are not desirable and should be avoided. This operation will not subdue your animal's mating drive, nor will it change your pet's aggressive attitude toward other males.

Spaying   Unless you are going to breed your female pet, it will be wise to have her spayed. This procedure is discussed in the "Diagnosis and Treatment" section of "Giving Birth."

Feeding   Proper feeding is indigenous to basic pet care. Both dogs and cats should be fed twice a day, and the amounts of food that you give your pet should be limited in order to keep its weight at a healthy level. After a male has been altered, or a female spayed, it should be fed less food because its body will require less to function normally. If you continue to give your animal the same amount of food as before the operation, it will usually eat it and may become obese.

Of course, it is most important to provide your pet with well-balanced and nutritious meals. Turn to the "Diagnosis and Treatment" section of "Vitamins and Food Requirements" for further information.

Cleaning Your Pet's Teeth   There are several ways that the animal-owner can help his or her pet to strengthen and clean its teeth. Turn to the "Diagnosis and Treatment" section of "Dental Care" for further information.

Treatment of Hairballs   Hairballs are most prevalent in long-haired cats and usually result from large amounts of dead hair ingested through the normal grooming process. Look for coughing and/or hacking similar to the "dry heaves"; an affected cat may also display clumps of hair in its stool. If left untreated, hairballs can cause constipation. Fortunately, the problem is easily alleviated. Simply coat the front paws with a thin layer of Vaseline or butter. As your animal licks its paws, the lubricant will be ingested and will help your pet to pass the hairballs through its stool.

BIRDS, FISH, AND TURTLES

Birds 185
Fresh-Water Tropical Fish 195
Turtles 203

This section includes special informational chapters on birds, fresh-water tropical fish and turtles.

Birds

Birds are usually pleasant pets, and their presence can brighten any household. While there are many different kinds of birds that people keep as pets, the information in this chapter will apply to all birds, unless otherwise stated.

Birds are normally confined in cages, but they can require even more attention than dogs and cats. Once a bird becomes ill, its condition can deteriorate rapidly and it can die a quick death. The best way to combat illness is through prevention, and this entails controlling your bird's environment, feeding it the proper foods, and proper grooming of the bird itself.

The Environment

Many of the potential problems that may threaten your bird can be effectively eliminated by a routine maintenance of its living quarters. Feeding receptacles should be frequently rinsed in warm water, and you should change the paper in the bottom of the cage whenever it becomes dirty. Keep the paper free of stray seeds, gravel, and toys, because anything that the bird finds while foraging (on the cage bottom) may be contaminated by droppings. If any of this material is ingested, it could cause the bird to suffer from bacterial or virus infections. You should also make sure that any perches or swings are not positioned over food or water dishes, for the same reason. It is also important to control the temperature of your pet's surroundings.

Keep your bird away from drafts and excessive cold or heat. Sudden drops in temperature can also be a source of danger. All varieties of caged birds have extremely sensitive respiratory systems, and what begins as a minor case of sniffles can quickly evolve into a secondary infection that threatens death. Never position the bird's cage near windows, doors, heating ducts, fans, air conditioners, etc. If you properly maintain your pet's environment, you have taken the first step toward ensuring its good health.

Nutrition Good nutrition will help keep your pet strong, and capable of staving off infection. There are some excellent commercial seed mixes that are available at your pet store, and these should form the basis of your bird's diet. Be sure to buy the mixture that has been prepared for your specific type of bird. For example, "Budgie Seed," "Finch Seed," and "Canary Seed," should be the staple nourishment for each respective type of bird. But birds need more than seeds to thrive, and they can eat many different food items.

Birds should have moulting food, fruit treat, condition food, and other variations, and these foods are usually sold at pet stores. Any of these specialized foods can be added to the basic seed mixture, and because birds like variety, they should be alternated on a daily basis. Birds can also be provided with fresh spinach, carrots, or celery greens, and they should be included in its diet once every few days. Grapes and oranges should be provided weekly or semiweekly, and large parrots can be given unsalted peanuts. It is also important to give your pet extra vitamins and minerals.

Vitamin supplements can be obtained from your pet store, and in some cases, from your veterinarian. They can be added to the bird's water or food, and they can be especially helpful during periods of stress, such as moulting and season changes. In addition, be sure to keep a cuttle bone or a mineral block in the cage at all times. Either of these items will fortify the bird's diet with needed calcium, and they will also help to trim its beak. If you want to supply your pet with extra protein, try "egg biscuits." This product is similar to croutons and is available at most pet shops.

Be sure to feed your bird at least once a day, even if the feeding receptable seems to be full. Birds (especially hook-beaked varieties) tend to eat only the inside meat of a seed, letting the complete shell fall back into the dish. For this reason, a wide, shallow dish is better than a narrow, deep one, as the rejected shells will form a layer over the uneaten seeds, making them difficult for the bird to reach.

WARNING   Never feed your bird table scraps or candy, because their digestive tracts are not suited to rich foods, and they may develop serious conditions as a result.

Grooming   While good grooming is not as vital to your pet's health as its environment and diet, your bird will naturally feel better with a regular trimming of its toe nails and beak. Cuttle bones or mineral blocks should sufficiently maintain the beak, but if your bird does develop an overgrowth, the only recourse is to trim it off.

Use a human nail clipper on smaller birds, but use a clipper meant for dogs on large parrots. Hold your bird firmly and trim only small amounts of beak at any one time. Be sure to trim the entire natural length of the beak, because the vein in the beak may lengthen as the beak grows longer. Next, cut the tip of the beak straight across, and shape the sides to look natural. You can also use the clippers on your pet's toe nails.

Hold the bird's feet up to the light so that you can see where the veins end. Then cut straight across each nail (never cut at an angle) and stay well away from the vein. If you do cut into the vein, the bird may begin to bleed badly. Many pet stores carry coagulants that will help to stop the flow of blood, and it is a good idea to have one on hand. Even if you are an experienced trimmer, you should be prepared to treat potentially dangerous bleeding. This coagulant can also be used on the bird's beak, in case you accidentally cut into the vein.

Unfortunately, even if you follow all of the preventative measures that have been outlined above, your bird can still get sick. However, most ailments can be successfully treated at home. If more than one bird shares the same cage, they will not normally have to be separated during treatment. Diseases in birds are almost always highly contagious, so birds in the same cage will usually benefit from the same medications. But you will have to act quickly. Birds have high metabolic rates, and this can cause any illness to be serious, and possibly even fatal. Early diagnosis and treatment are a must! You will usually recognize when your pet is ill, because sick birds often display an assortment of general symptoms.

Look for ruffled or puffed-out plumage, dull, half-closed eyes, and labored breathing. The bird may lose its appetite and become listless. It can stand on one leg, or squat unnaturally on its perch. These are symptoms, and not diseases. If your pet displays any of these indicators, you should take immediate action. Raise the temperature in its cage to 80 or 85 degrees Farenheit, and coax the bird to eat.

The temperature can be raised by placing a forty-watt light bulb near the cage or by placing a heating pad (on low) over or under the cage. You can also move the cage into a warm room, covering all but one side with a lightweight and lightly colored fabric. Once you are sure the bird is warm, try to get it to eat. Offer it its favorite foods. You can try nestling food, bread that has been soaked in boiled skim milk, or egg biscuits. Some sick birds like fruit or greens. If you have a hooked-beak bird, you can also try peanut butter. If the bird still refuses to eat, try to hand feed it. Each day your bird goes without eating, it becomes less likely to survive.

Once you have brought your pet out of immediate danger, you should observe it closely to determine which condition (or disease) is making it sick. Do not bring your bird (especially smaller birds) to the veterinarian.* The stress involved in making such a trip can be fatal for a bird already weakened by illness. Here is a list of common ailments, including their specific symptoms and treatment.

Colds   Birds can contract colds just as people do, but while the symptoms are similar, these colds are not contagious to humans. Look for sneezing or coughing, and a runny nose. These symptoms may not be severe, but in birds there is no such thing as a minor cold. Without prompt treatment, your bird may die. But most colds can be easily eliminated with antibiotics and inhalants.

Sulfamethazine, Erythromycin, and Tetracycline can be purchased in most pet stores and are usually effective in treating colds. But Tetracycline should only be used in the event that the other two fail because it is a much harsher drug. Be sure to administer the exact dosage that is recommended on the product's label. Too much medicine can hurt your bird, while too small an amount will probably have little affect on your pet's condition. If one antibiotic fails to kill the cold, try another, but never use more than one type at a time.

In addition to antibiotics, birds with colds will almost always benefit from inhalants. Commercial inhalants can be obtained at pet stores, and you should follow the instructions on the product's label. You can also use Vicks VapoRub. Smear a small amount of the rub on a tissue and place the medicated tissue in the bottom of your pet's cage. For maximum results, always keep your bird's cage covered, when you use any kind of inhalant.

Pneumonia   Birds can get pneumonia whenever they are exposed to excessive heat or cold, but the biggest cause of this condition is untreated

*Unless he or she has specifically advised you to do so.

colds. If you treat your bird's cold quickly, you can almost always prevent pneumonia. Many of the symptoms are the same as those associated with colds, but they are often more severe. Affected birds can also wheeze, shiver, and exhibit great difficulty in breathing. If your pet contracts this dangerous condition, treat it in the same way you would treat a cold—with antibiotics and inhalants.

Constipation

A constipated bird will strain and struggle while attempting to pass stool. It may also be listless and inactive. This disorder can be caused by digestive upsets, a poor diet, or colds. Treat this condition with a laxative and make sure that the bird has access to plenty of fresh greens. Do not use human laxatives because they are generally too harsh for birds. You can obtain special preparations from your pet store, and you should follow the instructions that are on the product's label.

Diarrhea

Diarrhea in birds is usually caused by improper diets or by various digestive problems. You should first attempt to treat this condition by using an anitbiotic that can be purchased from your pet store. Erythromycin is usually effective, but if the diarrhea fails to improve, you should try a stronger antibiotic like Tetracycline. If your pet still fails to respond, use a mild laxative (also from your pet store). Administer the laxative for two days, and then discontinue its usage. This may sound contrary, but diarrhea is the body's way of flushing impurities out of the digestive system, and laxatives aid in this cleansing.

Enteritis

This condition is highly contagious in birds, and can be extremely dangerous. This is one of the few times that birds in the same cage must be separated, unless they all appear to have the disease. The symptoms are diarrhea, rapid weight loss, and weakness characterized by drooping head and wings. The bird may also wobble or lurch forward on its perch. Enteritis is always caused by unclean living conditions, so keep your bird's cage clean. If your pet does develop this illness, treat it with antibiotics that are available at your pet store.

Regurgitation Regurgitation is normally a part of courtship behavior, and birds without companions will regurgitate erratically. While this condition can be somewhat disconcerting to the owner, it is not usually indicative of a serious problem. Sometimes a regurgitating bird will have a mild digestive disorder, but this will usually clear up by itself. If after one or two days your bird continues to regurgitate, add a small amount of baking soda to its drinking water. This is usually an effective treatment for digestive problems.

Feather Plucking Feather plucking is usually caused by boredom. Provide your bird with toys or a mirror. You can also try leaving your television or radio on whenever you leave the premises. Of course, the most satisfactory solution is to give your pet a companion. In some cases, feather plucking can result from a poor diet. Check your bird's menu against the requirements prescribed in the section on nutrition, and adjust accordingly.

Clogged Oil Gland All varieties of birds have an oil gland at the base of their tails. This gland distributes oil all over their feathers whenever they preen themselves and helps to keep them in a sleek and beautiful condition. When the gland clogs, the area around the tail will appear inflamed. This condition is not as serious as others, and it can be treated quickly and easily. Put a few drops of mineral oil on the affected duct, and apply light pressure with the pad of your thumb to ease any dry, clogging substance out.

Bumblefoot This condition will generally result from too much rich food in the bird's diet. After a while, fatty deposits will begin to accumulate on the bird's legs and feet, underneath their protective scales. These deposits will cause the bird to exhibit pain and distress as it tries to bend its toes or grip its perch. In milder cases, you can give your pet a blood tonic (available at pet stores) and correct its diet. But if the condition is severe, or if the bird's pain continues after treatment, you should consult your veterinarian.

French Moult French moult is a dangerous condition that can cause your bird to have difficulty in flying. It is always caused by a poor or improper diet. One of the symptoms is frequent shedding. Another is an abnormal regrowth of the bird's major flight and tail feathers. The bird will shed and regrow excessively, often resulting in an unattractive change in its appearance. This condition must be treated promptly, or it can shorten your pet's life by sapping its energy. Purchase a blood tonic from your pet store and administer it by following the directions on the label. More importantly, correct your bird's diet immediately.

Lumps
Lumps on the chest, abdomen, and wings are fairly common in larger parrots, and they are usually tumors or abscesses. If your parrot has a lump, it should be examined by your veterinarian. Benign or fatty tumors can be surgically removed in a relatively easy operation. But if the tumor is cancerous, surgery is useless because the disease is always fatal.

Fleas and Mites
External parasites are uncomfortable, and affected birds will usually show their distress. Sometimes you can see these parasites on the bird's body, but even if you cannot, the other symptoms should be easy to spot. Infested birds will scratch, fidget, and engage in frequent and violent preening. They can suffer from insomnia, and they may also begin to pluck out their feathers in an attempt to remove the source of irritation.

The most serious infestation is from a particular variety of mite that attacks the beak, cere, leg, and foot area. The affected regions of the bird's body will be inflamed and crusted. It is important to eliminate this parasite quickly, before the condition becomes severe. Many pet stores offer a mite killer that can be painted directly onto the affected area. Follow the directions on the label, but be sure to keep the medication away from your pet's eyes and mouth.

All of the other fleas and mites can be eliminated with insecticide bird sprays that are available at your pet store. Follow the instructions carefully and be sure to use only insecticides that are meant for birds. Continue to use this medication throughout the entire time period that is specified on the label, even if the parasites appear to be gone. If the condition does not improve, or if any of the symptoms are unusually severe and continue to persist, you should consult your veterinarian.

Broken Bones

Most of the broken bones in household birds occur in their legs or wings, and the fracture will be either simple or compound. A simple fracture is when a bone has broken into two pieces, both of which remain underneath the bird's skin. But compound fractures are visible, because the broken ends of the bone will have pushed through the skin. In either case, the bird will exhibit pain, and will usually be unable to bear any weight on the injured leg. Both types of fracture should be treated promptly, but compound breaks can be extremely serious.

If you have diagnosed a compound fracture, you should see your veterinarian. Do not attempt to splint the bone, as that may aggravate the bird's condition. Your veterinarian will know what to do. In some cases, the leg will have to be amputated. This is not as serious as it sounds, because caged birds can adapt quite nicely after losing a limb. Do not attempt to amputate the leg yourself.

If the leg is torn or mangled, it may also require amputation, even if the break is not compound. See your veterinarian.

Simple breaks can be treated at home, often with great success. The normal healing period is ten to twelve days, but severe breaks may take a little longer. Remove all but one perch from your pet's cage, and position the remaining perch fairly close to the bottom of the cage. If more than one bird resides in the cage, the others should be removed while the injured bird is healing. Be sure to put all food and water dishes within easy reach of the remaining perch, but not directly underneath it because this might cause the food and water to become contaminated by droppings. You will also have to monitor your bird's activity.

Put the cage in a quiet area of your house and keep it covered. This will discourage any unnecessary movement. If your bird still insists on climbing, turn the lights off and pull the shades of your windows down, until it becomes calm. Fractures must be rested in order to heal. If your bird has a broken wing, treat it in the same way as a broken leg.

Fresh-Water Tropical Fish

Fresh-water fish* can be enjoyable and fascinating to watch. They should be kept in an aquarium, and they normally need only a minimum of care to thrive. While there are several diseases that affect them, they can be treated at home, usually with great success. Sometimes these diseases are caused by introducing a sick fish into the tank, but more often, the very water that your fish live in will also be their greatest source of danger.

All of the disease organisms that attack fish are already present in their water. Fungi, parasites, viruses, and bacteria are an integral part of the chemical composition that makes up water. Fortunately, water also contains other bacteria that help the fish to

*There are two kinds of tropical fish that owners can keep—salt-water fish and fresh-water fish. But according to a recently conducted survey, more than 97 percent of North American fish-owners have opted to keep fresh-water fish, so this chapter will be strictly for them. If you are among the tiny minority of owners that keep salt-water fish, you can obtain a good book on their care and special problems from your pet store.

hold these disease organisms in check. But these bacteria must build into strong cultures in order to be effective. When the ratio of disease organisms to protective cultures goes out of balance, the fish can suffer stress. When fish are stressed, their natural defenses can be too busy to help ward off illness. This process of building up cultures is called the nitrogen cycle, and it begins when you first set up the aquarium.

The Nitrogen Cycle and the Break-In Period

An accumulation of ammonia results from the waste products of fish, and this ammonia is highly toxic. When the level of ammonia becomes excessive, the fish will die. But the nitrogen cycle, effected through the aquarium's filter, will change this ammonia into relatively harmless acid through three bacterial stages. The first stage changes the ammonia into nitrite which is still highly toxic. The second stage changes the nitrite into nitrate, which is not nearly as toxic as ammonia or nitrite. The final step changes the nitrate into acid. This constantly repeating process builds up strong bacterial cultures that help fish to fight off illness. If the nitrogen cycle is upset at any stage, the fish are in danger.

When a new aquarium is set up, it has no strong bacterial cultures, and the nitrogen cycle will be somewhat ineffective without one. It takes approximately twenty-one days for the culture to build up to the appropriate size, and this period of time is aptly named the break-in period. During this period, the population of your tank should be severely limited to a few fish. If you have too many fish, the unchecked ammonia can become excessive and kill them. Once the break-in period is over, you can gradually increase the population until there is about one inch of fish to every gallon of water. But do not add fish too quickly. The tank should not be fully populated until after the first six weeks of operation.

When the nitrogen cycle is functioning properly, the acid from the nitrate will begin to accumulate in the tank. High acidity can also threaten your fish, so you will have to control the acid level by routinely changing twenty-five percent of your aquarium's water. In most cases, a once-a-month change will be sufficient, but you will have to act sooner if it becomes necessary. You can test the acid (pH) level in your aquarium with a test kit that can be purchased at your pet store.

As long as the nitrogen cycle continues to function, your fish should be relatively safe. But if any of the bacterial stages break down, your fish can become stressed, and they may develop various symtpoms of disease. Because of the confining nature of aquariums, most diseases in fish are highly contagious, so you will have to act quickly. As soon as one fish displays any symptoms, you will have to treat the entire population. But before you administer a medication for any specific disease, check your water quality. If the chemistry is unbalanced, correct it, and the symptoms will usually vanish.

In some cases, bad water quality will cause conditions that are directly related to the specific stage that has broken down. These conditions are called ammonia poisoning, nitrite poisoning, and nitrate poisoning. They cause easily recognizable symptoms, and they can be quickly corrected by restoring the chemical balance. Here are the symptoms for each of these conditions, and how to treat them.

Ammonia Poisoning
When the nitrogen cycle breaks down before the ammonia has been changed into nitrite, the ammonia will continue to accumulate until it poisons the fish. The symptoms are easy to spot. Look for red, inflamed gills, labored breathing, and listlessness. Affected fish can also gasp at the top of the aquarium and fold their fins into their bodies. If this condition is left untreated, your fish will die. But before you can treat it, you must determine the cause.

Ammonia poisoning is usually caused by overcrowding the aquarium, overfeeding the fish, or by a faulty filter that stalls the nitrogen cycle in the first stage. If the cause is overcrowding, remove at least one-third of the population and put them into a separate tank. If you are overfeeding your fish, cut the amount of food down until all of it can be easily consumed in two or three minutes, and feed your fish only twice a day. If your aquarium has a faulty filter, it must be repaired or replaced. In addition, all three of these causes require a partial water change.

Depending on the severity of the poisoning, remove one-third to one-half of the aquarium's water, and replace it with fresh, uncontaminated water from your bathroom or kitchen tap.* After three days, change another third of the water, and continue to do so every three to five days, or until the symptoms are no longer present.

WARNING Do not put medications into your aquarium because they can destroy the bacterial culture that aids the cycle. This can result in a bad case of ammonia poisoning. All of the various fish medications except for Malachite Green (used to treat ick) should be administered in a separate tank. If you do contaminate your aquarium with medicine, you will have to break it down completely and give all of the parts a thorough cleaning. After all traces of the medication have been scrubbed out, you can set the tank up again; but be sure to start with very few fish. You will need to go through the normal break-in period before the entire population can be restored.

Nitrite Poisoning Nitrite poisoning can be extremely difficult to differentiate from ammonia poisoning, because the symptoms are exactly the same. Fortunately, the various causes and their specific treatments are also the same.

Nitrate Poisoning Nitrate poisoning is always caused by letting an aquarium go for long periods of time without partial water changes. It is often accompanied by a severe drop in the pH resulting in water with a very high acid content. Too much acid can be dangerous in itself, so you should correct the poisoning as soon as possible. The symptoms are obvious. Affected fish will have bloody lines in their tails and fins, and a cloudy film will be covering their eyes. They can also shudder. In some cases, the poisoning will cause an outbreak of other conditions, such as ick, fin and tail rot, and fungus. Fortunately, nitrate poisoning is very easy to treat.

*Whenever you effect a partial water change, be sure to add dechlorination drops. These drops can be purchased at your pet store, and you should follow the directions on the label. But never use these drops when setting up a new tank or effecting a total water change.

Simply change half of the water in your aquarium, and continue to change one-third of the water every three to five days, for as long as it is necessary. Do not treat your fish for any of the specific diseases that may develop from the poisoning. Once the water chemistry has been corrected, the symptoms of these diseases should disappear. Also, do not use Sodium Bicarbonate to rectify the pH. The acid content will adjust itself, once the water quality has been balanced.

WARNING   If you are using an undergravel filter, it can occasionally malfunction and affect the water, causing an anaerobic condition to develop. These conditions are extremely dangerous to fish, and they should be corrected immediately. The water in your aquarium will become cloudy and odorous, and your fish will begin to die. This condition results from "dead spots," or bypasses in the gravel, that prevent the filter from purifying the water. When this happens, food and waste begin to rot in the gravel, fermenting rather than degrading. This process sends off methane and carbon sulfate gases into the water, and both of these gases are deadly to fish. Once you diagnose an anaerobic condition, the only recourse is to break down your aquarium and start from scratch. You will have to use new water, clean gravel, and employ another break-in period.

Conditions   In some cases, the symptoms of diseases can continue to persevere
and Diseases   even after the water chemistry has been restored to a proper balance. When this happens, the condition will have to be treated with medication. Administer all medication (except Malachite Green) in a separate aquarium, and be sure to treat the entire population of fish. Here is a list of the common conditions that can affect fresh-water fish, including their symptoms and treatment.

Ick   Ick is a parasite that manifests itself as white spots on the body, tail, fins, and eyes of affected fish. Your fish will be most susceptible to this parasite during periods of high stress, like a transfer to a new aquarium, or whenever they are subjected to drastic changes in temperature. If this parasite is diagnosed early, it is easily controlled. Purchase a container of Malachite Green from your pet store, and follow the directions that are on the product's label. This is the only drug that can be administered while the fish are still in their regular aquarium, because it will not harm the bacterial culture.

Curved Spine
Curved spines can be easily seen in the affected fish. They are most often the result of birth defects and are very common among livebearers. Fry suffering from curvature of the spine should be destroyed immediately, because even if the fish survives into adulthood, the condition will worsen with age.

Overgrown Tail and Fins
The overgrowth of tail and fins results from improper nourishment when the fish is young. It is quite common in veiltail angels and fancy guppies. The body structure of affected fish becomes frail and stunted, even though the tail and fins continue to grow. The fish will be unattractive and out of proportion. Affected fish can also have great difficulty in swimming, and eventually they will develop curvature of the spine. You can correct this condition by removing the excess growth with a pair of scissors.

In the case of a guppy, net the fish and pick it up by the edge of the tail (the part that is to be cut off). Cut straight across the tail, but be sure to hold the fish over the open aquarium. When the cut has been completed, the fish will fall safely into the water. The process is exactly the same for angel fish, but it can be performed on the dorsal and pectoral fins, as well. Never hold your fish by its body, or the protective slime will come off in your hands.

Fungus
The incidence of fungus in fresh-water fish is rarer than commonly suspected, because parasitic infections (like ick) are often mistakenly diagnosed as fungus. The condition is caused by unclean water, and in order to treat it, you will have to be able to differentiate fungus from parasitic infections. Look for white, cottony blotches with wispy, threadlike appendages on the bodies, eyes, and mouths of affected fish. Once you spot this condition, you can treat it with a

partial water change. Continue to change the water in three-day periods until the fungus clears up.

Damaged Air Bladder

A damaged air bladder is indicated whenever a fish swims upside down, sideways, or backwards. In some cases, a fish will display this same behavior when it is disoriented, for example, if it is suddenly moved from darkness to bright light. But in these cases, the fish will return to normal behavior as soon as it becomes reoriented to its environment. If it continues to swim abnormally, it almost certainly suffers from a damaged air bladder. There is no treatment for this condition, and all fish that are afflicted should be destroyed.

Dropsy

Dropsy is peculiar to livebearers, especially mollies. The symptoms are ruffled scales, drooping fins, and listlessness. This condition is highly contagious, and it can only be treated with an anitbiotic. But antibiotics are uncertain—sometimes they cure the disease, and sometimes they kill the fish. Moreover, antibiotics destroy the bacterial culture that aids the nitrogen cycle, so they must be administered in a separate tank. For these reasons, the cure can be worse than the disease, and it is highly recommended that affected fish be destroyed, rather than treated. But if you do decide to treat your fish, isolate it (or them) in a different aquarium, and administer either Erythromycin or Tetracycline. Both of these antibiotics are available in your pet store, and you should follow the instructions that are on the label.

Fin and Tail Rot

Fin and tail rot can be seen on affected fish. Look for wedge-shaped spaces in the fins and tails. This condition is bacterial in nature, and it can be controlled with partial water changes. If the condition is very severe, you can treat it with the same antibiotics that are used to treat dropsy. But this is not recommended for the same reasons that have already been stated in the section on dropsy. If you do use antibiotics, isolate all afflicted fish in a separate tank, and follow the instructions that are on the label.

Sunken Stomachs   In almost all cases, sunken stomach results from an intestinal infection or starvation. The condition can be seen by looking at the abdominal region of the fish. It will be clearly hollowed into the body. You can correct this condition with partial water changes, and consistent twice-a-day feedings.

WARNING   In rare cases, a sunken stomach can be a symptom of tuberculosis. If your fish does not respond after several days of treatment, it probably suffers from this condition. If so, it will have to be destroyed, as there is no cure for tuberculosis.

Pop Eye   Pop eye is a bacterial infection that causes swelling behind the eyes of fish. The pressure from this swelling causes the eyes to be forced out of the head, and the fish will appear to be pop-eyed. This infection is more stubborn than fin and tail rot, and it must be treated with antibiotics. Use either Erythromycin or Tetracycline. Both of these medications can be purchased at your pet store, and you should follow the directions that are on the product's label. Be sure to treat all affected fish in a separate aquarium.

Turtles

Turtles are generally hearty animals, and they can make enjoyable pets. Many breeds have life spans of over thirty years, and if you house and feed your turtle properly, it will rarely be ill.

Housing   Depending on your type of turtle, it will live either in an aquarium (water turtles) or in a terrarium (land turtles). Both kinds of turtles need five gallons of living space for every inch and a half of their length. Since your turtle will not be less than four inches long,* your aquarium or terrarium should be no smaller than fifteen gallons. For each turtle (of the same size) that shares the tank, add an extra ten gallons of space. The tank will also have to have the right shape.

Never buy "high" tanks for the purpose of housing turtles. Turtles

*Turtles are measured from the front of their shells to the back. A recently passed national law forbids the sale of turtles that are under four inches long, because of a high incidence of Salmonella in small turtles.

need surface space in order to thrive. It is especially important for land turtles to have plenty of area to move around in because they have a tendency to sit listlessly in cramped quarters. This often causes them to develop painful sores on their plastrons (the underside of the shell) that are similar to bed sores in humans. So make sure that the requisite number of gallons for living space is mostly wide, and not high. You will also want to make your pet's tank a comfortable place to live in.

Aquariums Water turtles need warm water, or they can become unhappy with their surroundings. Fill the aquarium with two to three inches of water, and maintain the temperature at approximately 75 degrees Farenheit by installing a hood light on the tank. You should also equip the tank with a glass lid to control the humidity. Next, you will have to give your turtle a dry area to rest.

A rock or plastic "island" must stick up out of the water or be suspended over it. This resting place must have sufficient dry area for the turtle to dry its entire body, including the plastron. Your pet should have easy access to this rock, and it should be able to climb on and off with a minimum of effort. But make sure that the rock has no rough spots or edges or the turtle may injure its plastron. Once you have attended to the turtle's needs, you can decorate the tank with live or plastic plants, smooth stones, or figurines. Do not use shells. When shells are placed in water, they trap debris and cause an imbalance in the water chemistry.

Terrariums Land turtles need a good surface to crawl on. Cover the bottom of the terrarium with pebbles, but do not use any gravel. Gravel has sharp edges that can irritate your turtle's plastron. Next, give your pet a source of water for bathing, swimming, and drinking. Sink a dish of water into the pebbles. The dish must be sufficiently shallow to allow the turtle to crawl in and out of it easily. If it is too deep, the turtle could fall in upside down and drown. You should also provide a dish that is large enough for the turtle to move around in comfortably. Be sure to change the water whenever it gets dirty, which is usually every four or five days.

Like aquariums, terrariums should have glass lids and hood lights to help control the humidity and the temperature. After the tank has been made suitable for living, you can decorate the surface area with plastic or live plants, smooth stones, figurines, or shells.

It is strongly recommended that owners equip their aquariums with undergravel or box filters. The undergravel filter can be hidden underneath the bottom surface, while the box filter must be placed on top. Either of these devices will help to keep the water free from impurities, but the box filter will require regular maintainence, while the undergravel filter does not.

Feeding   Water turtles should be fed in an area separate from the aquarium that they live in, or you may end up doing a lot of unnecessary cleaning. The "turtle bowls" that are sold in pet shops make excellent feeding containers. So do dish tubs and wide, plastic garbage cans. Fill the feeding area with two or three inches of water, and make sure that the water has been warmed to approximate the temperature in the aquarium. Then move your pet into the feeding area and feed it. After the turtle has finished eating, you can move it back into the aquarium, and simply rinse out the feeding bowl. If you do not use a separate container to feed your pet, the water in the aquarium will frequently become dirty, and you will have to clean it. Using one of the filter devices will help, but you will still have extra work to do. Land turtles can be fed by placing their food on top of the pebbled surface.

Turtles do not need to eat every day, so feed your pet every other day. After the turtle begins to eat, let it continue to eat until it stops on its own. Make sure that your turtle is eating regularly, but be careful not to overfeed it.

Turtle Foods   Water turtles should be fed meal worms, earthworms, crickets, and other insects. You can also give them raw fish, bananas, lettuce, spinach, cucumber, and zucchini. Make sure that their food has been broken up into small and manageable pieces. Worms, minnows, and insects can be purchased at bait stores, and flying insects can be caught by hanging out a white sheet at night and shining a light on it.

Land turtles can eat anything that water turtles eat, but they also like tomatoes, grapes, cantaloupe, and other fruits. As a general rule, water turtles prefer insects, whereas land turtles would rather eat fruits and vegetables.

In addition to the proper foods, both kinds of turtle will benefit from extra vitamins and either bone meal or powdered calcium. You should mix these supplements into their food everytime they eat. You should also place a calcium block into their water supplies and let it remain there at all times. The supplements and calcium block can be purchased at your pet store.

WARNING Never feed your turtle hamburger and avoid commercially packaged turtle food unless it has been fortified with extra vitamins and minerals. Hamburger is oily, and it will coat your pet's digestive tract; this will prevent your turtle from absorbing essential nutrients. Many of the commercially prepared turtle foods have little nutritional value. Look on the product's label. If it does not proclaim additional vitamins and minerals, do not feed it to your pet.

When Your Turtle Is Sick Pet owners should know how to give their turtles medicine, before they begin to treat its condition. Never administer medication orally. This involves prying the turtle's mouth open and forcing the liquid down their throats with an eyedropper. Even if the jaw were not badly bruised in the process, the turtle may choke, or the medication may travel into its lungs. In either case, the result can be fatal. All medications should be added to the turtle's water supply, mixed into its food, or applied directly to the problem area whenever possible.

Fortunately, turtles almost never get sick, especially if they are properly housed and fed. While there are a few diseases that turtles are susceptible to, most are not fatal. But they can be uncomfortable, so it is important to begin treatment as soon as possible. If more than one turtle is sharing the same tank, treat them all, even if only one exhibits the symptoms for any particular condition. Because turtles live in a confined environment, most of the common conditions are highly contagious. Even if one or more of your pets does not exhibit any symptoms, they will probably develop them within a few days, and advance treatment is generally good prevention. But be very careful whenever you administer antibiotics. Always follow the recommended dosage on the label exactly because overdoses can be fatal.

Here is a list of the common ailments, including their specific symptoms and modes of treatment.

Refusal To Eat   Turtles may refuse to eat whenever they are ill, or when their environmental temperature becomes too cold. Alternatively, a turtle may refuse to eat for no apparent reason at all. Regardless of the cause, this condition should always be treated in the same way. Gradually raise the temperature in their tank to approximately 78 degrees Farenheit. This should be done slowly, over a twenty-four hour period. You should also add vitamins to their water supply, including the water in their feeding area. Do everything possible to coax your pet into eating. Offer it its favorite foods. But do not let the food sit in the water (or on the pebbles) for long periods of time. If your turtle does not eat within thirty minutes, remove the food and try again.

If your turtle is not eating because it is ill, you may have to treat its condition before it will begin to eat again. But in most cases, the turtle will regain its appetite within a short period of time.

Attempting To Hibernate   If you let the temperature in your turtle's tank drop below 70 degrees Farenheit, it may attempt to hibernate. But many turtles in captivity do not hibernate effectively, they merely starve to death. The symptoms of this condition are listlessness, refusal to eat, and the appearance of being asleep. Follow the treatment procedures that are outlined in "Refusal to Eat," and your pet will usually regain its vitality within a few days.

Pneumonia   Turtles can get pneumonia, just like humans. Although the symptoms are similar, this disease in turtles is not caused by low humidity or by abrupt changes in the turtle's environmental temperature. The early symptoms will usually be recognizable, and you should always act quickly. Look for listlessness, refusal to eat, respiratory distress, and a discharge from the turtle's nostrils. If your pet displays these symptoms, raise its tank temperature to 78 degrees Farenheit, and give it an antibiotic (available at your pet store). Be sure to initiate treatment immediately, because pneumonia is almost always fatal if left untreated.

Constipation   Constipation will usually occur only in land turtles. If your pet struggles and strains while attempting to pass stool, it is probably constipated. The treatment is simple. Let the turtle sit in an inch or two of warm water (79 degrees Farenheit) for approximately forty-five minutes, and the condition will usually clear up.

Fungus   Fungus manifests itself as greyish-white spots on the turtle's body, and on its eyes. The treatment consists of administering aquarium fungicides. These fungicides can be purchased at your pet store, and even though they are generally indicated for tropical fish, they are also effective when used on turtles. Follow the instructions on the product's label, and the fungus should subside.

Soft Shell   Soft shell is caused by a deficiency of calcium in the turtle's diet. You will be able to feel this condition by gently pushing your finger against the turtle's shell. Always push into the rim of the shell, because if you push into the center, you may seriously injure your pet. To treat soft shell, simply correct the deficiency. Mix large amounts of bone meal or calcium powder (from pet store) into your turtle's water supply and food. Even after the shell becomes hard again, continue to supply an adequate amount of calcium in its diet.

Inflamed Eyes   Inflamed eyes are due to a bacterial infection that is generated from unclean living conditions. Look down on your turtle. If its eyes are swollen and puffed out from its head, it is probably suffering from inflamed eyes. You can treat this condition by adding an antibiotic (from pet store) like Aureomycin or Erythromycin to the turtle's water supply, or your veterinarian can prescribe a penicillin ointment that can be applied directly to the turtle's eyes.

But most importantly, give your pet's home a thorough cleaning and be sure to keep it clean at all times.

Damaged Plastron

Unclean living conditions and rough surface areas can damage your pet's plastron. As it crawls through and over rough material and rubble, sharp and uneven edges can cause bruises and sores. Once the plastron becomes sore or pitted, it should be treated with an undiluted fungicide that can be purchased at your pet store. Apply the fungicide directly into the turtle's sores. But the best cure is prevention. See that your pet's home is kept clean and do not allow your turtle to sit in its own waste. Be sure to replace all sharp rocks and gravel with smoother rocks and pebbles.

Broken Skin

Cuts and similar injuries will usually be visible to the owner's eye. They should be cleaned and treated with a penicillin ointment or a fungicide. The ointment will have to be prescribed by your veterinarian; the fungicide can be obtained at your pet store.

Index

Abortion, spontaneous, 110
Abrasions, 9, 50–51, 141
Acute pruritis, 27
Air bladder, damage of, 201
Allergies, 23, 53, 102, 113, 116, 117
Aloe plant, 43, 45, 137, 138, 141
Alpha-Keri, 118
Altering, 80, 180
Ammonia poisoning, 197–98
Antibiotics, 49, 189, 190, 201, 202, 208
  See also specific antibiotics.
Appetite:
  calici virus and, 26, 111
  heat and, 17
  rabies and, 26, 112
  respiratory infections, 22, 25, 109, 111
  tapeworms and, 20
  turtles and, 207
Aquarium, turtles and, 203, 204.
  See also Fresh-water tropical fish.
Arthritis, 31, 129–30, 161–62
Ascarids. *See* Roundworms.
Aspirin, 53–54, 103
  arthritis and, 162
  burns and, 138
  cats and, 54, 135
  dental care and, 145
  dosages, 135–36, 142
  fractures, 135–36
  respiratory infections, 155
  wounds, 142
Asthma, 23, 102–3
Aureomycin, 208

Bactine, 49, 140
Bad breath, 13, 52
Bandages, 49–50, 122–23
Bathing, 118, 176–79
Beak, of bird, 187–88
Birds, 185–94
  diseases, 188–93
  environment, 185–86
  fractures, 193–94
  grooming, 187–88
  nutrition, 186–87
  obtaining, 172
Birth. *See* Reproduction.
Bleeding:
  cuts and, 9, 49
  heat and, 17, 81
  internal, 38
  lacerations and, 9
  serious wounds and, 51, 141
  in stool, 14, 20, 21, 70, 71–72, 147
Blisters, burns and, 7, 8

Bones:
  chewing habits and, 64–65, 128
  rickets and, 30
  See also Fractures
Bowel movement. *See* Stool.
Brain damage, 104, 108
Broken bones. *See* Fractures.
Bruise, 10, 51, 53, 141
Bumblefoot, 191
Burns:
  chemical, 45
  diagnosis and treatment, 41–47, 137–38
  electrical, 7–8, 42–43, 46–47, 137
  friction, 8, 44–45, 137–38
  symptoms, 7–8
  thermal, 8, 43–44, 137–39
Burrow's solution, 44, 45, 117, 137, 138
Butter, 118, 158

Calamine lotion, 120, 141
Calcium, 129–30, 208
Calici virus, 23, 26, 104, 106, 111
Cancer, of skin, 27–28, 36
Canine distemper, 21, 24–25, 94, 104, 108
Cardiac arrest, 7, 42
Castration, 180
Casts, 39–40
Cat distemper, 25, 106, 110–11
Cats:
  aspirin and, 54, 135
  bathing, 176–77
  bones and, 64–65, 128
  constipation, 55–56, 57, 68
  dental problems, 12
  diseases, 21, 23, 25–26, 91, 94, 98, 104, 106, 111–12, 130
  hair trimming, 180
  heat, 82
  milk and, 57, 130–31
  nails, 179
  reproduction, 17–18
  teething, 63–64
Cecum, 95, 96
Cerebellar hypoplasia, 110–11
Certo, 129–30, 161
Chemical burn, 45
Chicken neck, cats and, 64–65, 128
Cholesterol, 130
Claws, dewing, 87
Clogged oil gland, 191
Coat:
  burns and, 47
  dry skin and, 28
  egg yolk and, 128
  heartworms and, 21, 96

Coat *(cont.)*
   internal parasites and, 20
   malnutrition and, 30
Coccidia, 21, 91, 97
Cockatoo, 172
Cold applications, 49, 50, 51, 122, 141, 159
Colds, 104, 154, 189
Colon, whipworm and, 21
Commercial foods, 126–27
Compound fracture, 6, 35, 193.
   See also Fractures
Concussion, 37–38
Congenital hip dysplasia, 89
Congestion, 26, 153–54
Constipation, 55–60, 63
   birds, 190
   cats, 55–56, 57, 58
   causes, 56–57
   complications, 59
   diagnosis and treatment, 55–56, 143–44
   symptoms, 11
   teeting and, 13
   turtles, 208
Contac, 154
Contractions. *See* Reproduction.
Contusions. *See* Bruises.
Convulsions:
   canine distemper, 25, 108
   internal parasites, 90
   rabies, 26, 113
   roundworm, 94
Coughing:
   canine distemper and, 25, 108
   dental problems and, 13
   heartworms, 21, 96
   hookworm and, 20
   respiratory infections, 22, 25, 26, 110
   treatment, 154–55
Cramps, 20, 94
Curved spine, 200
Cuts, 8–9, 48–50, 52–53, 140–41
   turtles, 209
Cystic ovaries, 82
Cysts, 120

Dandruff, 30, 158
Dehydration:
   calici virus, 26, 111
   constipation and, 59
   diagnosis of, 60
   respiratory infections, 25, 26
   whipworms, 95
Demodetic mites, 16, 76
Dental care:
   broken teeth, 65–66
   causes, 61-62
   chewing habits, 63–65, 67
   cleaning, 62–63, 67
   diagnosis and treatment, 12–13, 61–67, 145

Dental care *(cont.)*
   foreign material removal, 66–67
   prevention, 62–63
   teething, 63–64
   teeth loss, 65
Depression:
   calici virus, 26, 111
   cat distemper, 110
   infectious canine hepatitis, 25
   Leptospirosis, 25, 109
   respiratory infections, 25
Diarrhea, 63, 68
   birds, 190
   blood in, 71–72, 147
   canine distemper and, 108
   cats and, 24, 25, 68, 69, 70, 71, 110
   coccidia, 21, 97
   contagion, 71
   diagnosis and treatment, 68–72, 146–47
   food supplements and, 128
   heartworms, 96
   hookworm, 20, 21, 70, 94–95
   intermittent, 71
   internal parasites, 19, 90, 91, 99
   Leptospirosis and, 25
   milk products, 57, 130
   oil and, 158
   roundworms and, 94
   symptoms, 11, 14
   teething, 13
   whipworms, 21, 70, 95
Diet:
   bruise or contusion and, 53
   constipation, 57
   diarrhea and, 68–69
   reproduction and, 83
   skin disorders, 116, 117, 118
   See also Nutrition.
Discharge, 13, 17, 18
   See also Eyes; Nasal discharge.
Disease, vaccination and, 104, 106, 107–8, 110, 111, 113
   See also specific diseases.
Distemper:
   canine, 21, 24–25, 94, 104, 108
   cat, 25, 106, 110–11
Domeboro tables, 44, 45, 117, 137, 138, 141
Drooling, 26, 112–13
Dropsy, 201
Drugs. *See* specific drugs.
Dry skin, 117–18, 158
Dumb rabies, 26, 112
Ear mites, 16, 76, 78
Ears
   cleaning, 178–79
   ear mites and, 16, 76, 78
Eczema, 27
Egg yolk, 128
Electrical burns, 7–8, 42–43, 46–47, 137
Encephalitis, 26, 113

Enteritis, 190
Erythromycin, 189, 190, 201, 202, 208
Exercise, 46
External parasites:
    diagnosis and treatment, 73–78, 117, 148–49
    fleas, 15, 74–75, 77, 120, 148
    grooming and, 174
    lice, 15, 75, 77, 148
    maggots, 15, 75, 149
    mange, 76, 77, 120
    mites, 16, 75, 76, 78, 149, 192–93
    symptoms of, 15–16
    ticks, 15, 75, 120, 148
Eyelids, 7, 21
Eyes:
    cleaning, 179
    concussion and, 37
    congestion, 25
    discharge from, 21, 24, 25–26, 108, 111
    infectious canine hepatitis and, 109
    Leptospirosis and, 109
    malnutrition and, 30
    runny, 22

Fats, 128
Feather plucking, 191
Feces. See Stool.
Feline enteritis. See Cat distemper.
Fertility. See Reproduction.
Fever:
    calici virus and, 26, 111
    distemper and, 24, 25, 108, 110
    hookworm and, 21
    infectious canine hepatitis and, 109
    rabies and, 26, 112
    respiratory infections and, 25, 26, 104, 109, 111
    steatitis, 31
Fin and tail rot, 201
Fins, of fish, 200
Fish. See Fresh-water tropical fish.
Flea-bite dermatitis, 74
Fleas, 15, 74–75, 77, 120, 148
    birds and, 192–93
    coccidia and, 97
    tapeworms and, 92
Food. See Nutrition.
Foot pads:
    burns on, 45
    canine distemper and, 25, 108
    cuts on, 52
Fractures:
    birds and, 193–94
    causes, 35–36
    compound, 6, 35, 193
    diagnosis and treatment, 35–40, 135–36
    pain and, 54
    simple, 6, 25, 35, 192–93
    swelling, 36–37
    symptoms, 5–6, 36, 142, 160

French moult, 191–92
Fresh-water tropical fish, 195–202
    ammonia poisoning, 197–98
    break-in period, 196
    diseases, 198–202
    medicine administration, 198, 199
    nitrogen cycle, 196–97
    water change, 196, 198, 199, 201, 202
Friction burns, 8, 44–45, 137–39
Full-service pet store, 169, 171–72
Fungicide, 208, 209
Fungus, 115, 200–201, 208
Furacin, 49, 140
Furious rabies, 26, 112

Gangrene, 47
Garlic, internal parasites and, 152
Gas, 71
Gestation. See Reproduction.
Gingivitis, 13, 61, 62
Glycerine suppository, 143
Grooming, 173–76
    bathing and, 176–79
    birds, 187–88
    full-service pet shop and, 169, 171–72
    hair trimming, 180
    nail trimming, 179
    skin disorders, 115
Growths. See Tumors.
Gums:
    burns and, 7, 8
    hookworm and, 20
    whipworms and, 21
    See also Dental conditions.

Hair:
    loss, 16
    trimming, 180
    See also Coat; Grooming.
Hairballs, 174, 181
Heart:
    electrical burns and, 42
    heartworms and, 21, 96–97
    internal parasites, 100
Heartworm, 21, 91, 96–97, 100
Heat. See Reproduction.
Hernia, 57
Hibernation, turtles and, 207
Hips, 39, 125
Hives, 23, 117
Hookworm, 20–21, 70, 91, 94–95, 99
Humidifier, 103
Hydrogen peroxide, 49, 140

Ice bag. See Cold applications.
Ick, 198, 199–200
Impaction. See Constipation.
Infection, 47, 52
    See also specific infections.
Infectious canine hepatitis, 25, 108–9

Infectious canine tracheobronchitis, 25, 104, 109–10
Infestation. *See* Internal parasites.
Inhalants, 189
Inoculation. *See* Vaccination.
Internal parasites, 90–100
  brain damage and, 100
  coccidia, 21, 91, 97
  contagion, 100
  diagnosis and treatment, 91–92, 99, 151–52
  grooming and, 174
  heartworm, 21, 91, 96–97, 100
  hookworm, 20–21, 70, 91, 94–95, 99
  milk and, 98
  pregnancy and, 80
  roundworms, 20, 90–91, 93–94
  tapeworms, 20, 90–91, 92–93
  toxoplasmosis, 21, 91, 98
  whipworm, 21, 70, 91, 95–96
  worming programs, 100
Iodine, 49, 140
Itching, 157

Jaundice, 25, 109
Jaws, broken, 38
Joints. *See* Sprains.

Kaopectate, 70, 131, 146
Kennel cough. *See* Infectious canine tracheobronchitis.
Kidneys, uremia and, 13, 62
Kitten ataxia, 110–11

Laceration, 9, 50, 52–53, 140–41, 144
Land turtles. *See* Turtles.
Laryngitis, 22, 102
Leptospirosis, 25, 109
Lesions, electrical burn and, 7
Lethargy. *See* Listlessness.
Lice, 15, 75, 77, 148
Ligaments, 124
Lightning, electrical burns and, 42
Limited-service pet store, 169
Limp, 5–6, 29
Lips:
  burns and, 7, 8
  hookworm and, 20
  whipworm and, 21
Listlessness:
  heartworms and, 21
  infectious canine hepatitis, 109
  pneumonitis, 26
  respiratory infections, 22
  roundworms and, 20
Litter. *See* Reproduction.
Livebearers, 201
Lumps. *See* Tumors.
Lungs, roundworm and, 20

Maggots, 15, 75, 149
Malachite Green, 198, 199, 200
Malnutrition, 30–31, 36
  See also Nutrition.

Mange, 76, 77, 120
Marrow bones, 64, 128
Medications. *See* specific medications.
Menopause, 89
Merthiolate, 49, 140
Meta-Mucil, 57, 143
Milk of bismuth, 131
Milk of magnesia, 58, 144
Milk products, 98, 130–31
Mineral oil, 58, 143–44, 178–79
Mites, 16, 75, 76, 78, 149
  birds and, 192–93
Mollies, dropsy in, 201
Mosquitos, heartworms and, 96
Mucous, infectious canine tracheobronchitis and, 25, 110
  See also Nasal discharge.
Mucous membranes:
  infectious canine hepatitis and, 25, 109
  shock and, 8, 42, 51
  whipworms and, 21

Nail trimming, 179
Nasal discharge:
  calici virus, 21, 111
  canine distemper, 24, 108
  coccidia and, 21
  dental problems and, 13
  hookworms, 21
  respiratory infections and, 22, 23, 25–26
Neutering, 180–81
Nitrate poisoning, 198–99
Nitrite poisoning, 198
Nitrogen cycle, fish and, 196–97
Nupercainol, 50, 141
Nursing, 86–87
Nutrition, 30–31
  arthritis, 129–30, 161–62
  birds, 186–87
  bones, 128
  cholesterol, 130
  feeding, 181
  malnutrition, 128–29, 130–31, 161–62
  turtles, 205–6
  See also Diet.

Ocular discharge. *See* Eyes.
Oils, 117–18, 128, 158
Oral discharge, dental problem and, 13
Oxygen, burns and, 42, 46–47

Panleucopenia. *See* Cat distemper.
Panting, heartworms and, 21, 96
Parainfluenza. *See* Infectious canine tracheobronchitis.
Paralysis, rabies and, 26, 113
Parasites, diarrhea and, 71
  See also External parasites; Internal parasites.
Paw. *See* Foot pad.
Pelvis, fractured, 6, 36
Penicillin, 208, 209
Pepto Bismol, 70, 131, 146

Perineal hernia, 57
Pet-care, 173–81
    See also specific aspects of pet care.
Pet store, 168–72
Plastron, 204, 209
Pneumonia, 104, 105
    birds and, 189–90
    canine distemper and, 25, 108
    internal parasites and, 90
    roundworms, 20, 93
    turtles and, 207–8
Pneumonitis, 26, 111–12
Poison ivy, 20
Pop eye, 202
Pregnancy. *See* Reproduction.
Pulmonary edema, 42
"Puppy worms." *See* Roundworms.
Pyometra, 81

Rabies, 24, 26, 107, 112–13, 115
Rash, 23
Regurgitation, 191
    See also Vomit.
Reproduction, 79–80
    altering, 80
    cat distemper and, 110
    claw dewing, 87
    complications, 85–86, 150
    contractions, 84
    diet, 83
    fertility, 82, 89
    gestation, 17, 80, 82–84, 88
    heat, 17–18, 79, 80–82, 87, 88, 89
    heredity and, 89
    internal parasites and, 80
    menopause, 89
    newborns and, 86–87, 88, 89
    nursing, 86–87
    spaying, 80, 81, 82
    symptoms, 17–18
    tail removal, 87
    whelping, 82–86, 88
Respiratory infections, 101–6
    aspirin, 103, 155
    cats and, 25–26
    congestion, 153–54
    contagion, 105–6
    coughing, 154–55
    electrical burns, 7
    fever, 104
    precautions against, 103, 105
    sinus conditions, 154
    symptoms, 22–23, 101–2
    treatment, 104, 113–14, 153–56
    vaccination and, 104, 106
    vaporizer, 103, 153
    See also specific diseases.
Rhinitis, 23, 102
Rhinotracheitis, 23, 25–26, 104, 111
Ribcage, sprain and, 125

Ribs, fractured, 38–39
Rickets, 30, 36, 129
Ringworm, 115, 117, 120
Roundworm, 20, 90, 91, 93–94

Salmonella, 203
Sarcoptic mange, 77, 120
Sarcoptic mites, 16, 76
Scratching, 15, 28, 118
Seborrhea, 28
Shampoo, 118, 177–78
Shedding, 119, 173–74
    birds and, 192
    See also Grooming.
Shock:
    burns and, 8, 42, 43, 137
    concussion and, 38
    fractured rib and, 38–39
    serious wound and, 51–52
    symptoms of, 8
    treatment, 8
Simple fractures, 6, 25, 192–93
    See also Fractures.
Sinus conditions, 23, 102, 103, 154
Sinutab, 103, 154
Skin disorders, 115–20
    bathing, 118
    causes, 115–16, 117
    contagion, 119–20
    dry skin, 117–18, 158
    growths, 120
    hives, 117
    hookworm, 99
    itching, 157
    shedding, 119
    symptoms, 27–28
    treatment, 116–18, 120, 157–58
    See also External parasites; Grooming.
Skulls, fractures of, 38
Sneezing, 22, 24, 26, 111
Snorting, pneumonitis, 26
Soap suppository, 57, 143
Solarcaine, 50, 117, 141, 157
Spaying, 80, 81, 82, 181
Specialty pet stores, 169–70
Splint, fracture and, 37
Sprains, 29, 121–25, 159–60
    See also Fractures.
Starch, 131
Steatitis, 31, 130
Stool. *See* Constipation; Diarrhea; Internal parasites.
Stool softener, 57, 143
Sugar, 130
Sulfamethazine, 189
Suppository, constipation and, 57
Sunken stomachs, 202
Surgery, 39, 120
Swallowing, rabies and, 26, 112–13, 114
Swelling, 50
    fractures and, 5, 6, 36–37

Swelling *(cont.)*
  sprains, 29, 122
  wounds, 9
Swollen glands, 22

Tail, 87, 124
  of fish, 200
Tapeworms, 20, 90–91, 92–93
Tartar, 12, 13, 62–64, 66–67
Teeth. *See* Dental care.
Teething, 13, 63–64
  coccidia, 97
  diarrhea and, 69, 70
  electrical burns and, 46
  food and, 128
Temperature, shock and, 8
  See also Fever.
Tendons, injury to, 124
Terrarium, turtles and, 203, 204
Tetracycline, 189, 190, 201, 202
Thermal burns, 8, 43–44, 137–39
Thirst, 13, 25, 62, 109
Thyroid gland, 116
Ticks, 15, 75, 120, 148
Tongue:
  calici virus and, 111
  ulcerations in, 26
Tonsils, 22, 102, 104
Tourniquet, 49
Toxoplasmosis, 21, 91, 98
Trauma, 8, 35–36, 44
Tropical fish. *See* Fresh-water tropical fish.
Tuberculosis, 202
"Tucked up" walk, 25
Tumors, 27–28, 120
  birds, 192
  fractures and, 36
Turtles:
  appetite loss, 207
  aquarium, 203–4
  diseases, 205–6, 207–9
  foods, 205–6
  hibernation, 207
  housing, 203–4
  land, 293, 204–5, 206, 208
  medication administration, 206
  plastrons, 204, 209
  salmonella in, 203

Turtles *(cont.)*
  terrarium in, 203, 204–5
  water, 203, 204, 205, 206
Twitching, 25, 108

Unguentine ointment, 50, 141
Unguentine plant. *See* Aloe plant.
Uremia, 13, 61, 62
Urine:
  heat and, 17
  infectious canine hepatitis and, 108–9
  Leptospirosis and, 109
  male cats, 180

Vaccination, 104, 106, 107–8, 110, 111, 113
Vaporizer, 103, 153
Vasectomies, 181
Vaseline, 49, 50, 141
Vermicides, 151
Veterinarian, 165–67, 171
Vick's VapoRub, 104, 153, 189
Virus. *See* specific viruses.
Vitamins:
  C, 104
  E, 44, 130, 141
  See also Nutrition.
Vomit:
  birds, 191
  cat distemper, 25, 110
  internal parasites, 90, 91
  Leptospirosis, 109
  roundworm, 20
  whipworms, 95
Vulva, 17, 81

Water turtles. *See* Turtles.
Weight loss, 20, 95, 96, 97
Wet dermatitis, 27
Wheezing, 23
Whelping. *See* Reproduction.
"Whiplash," 125
Whipworm, 21, 70, 91, 95–96
Worms, 20–21
  See also Internal parasites.
Wounds, 9–10, 48–54, 140–42
  See also specific wounds.

X-rays, 37

Yellow fat disease. *See* Steatitis.